MORE
EASY BEANS

Quick and tasty bean, pea and lentil recipes

Trish Ross and Jacquie Trafford

D0009720

BIG BEAN PUBLISHING

Big Bean Publishing
Suite 201-1508 Mariners Walk
Vancouver, British Columbia
Canada V6J 4X9

CANADIAN CATALOGUING IN PUBLICATION DATA
822-6838

Ross, Trish
  More Easy Beans

ISBN 0-9698162-1-9

1. Cookery (Beans) 2. Cookery (Peas) 3. Cookery (Lentils)
I. Trafford, Jacquie II. Title
TX803.B4R68 1996 641.6'565 C96-910818-4

Text design and typesetting: Stubblejumper Communications
Text illustrations: Neil Thacker
Cover design: Val Speidel
Cover photograph: Clinton Hussey
Food stylist: Wayne Palmer-Haenisch
Printed and bound in Canada
Printed on acid-free paper

Contents

Acknowledgements

To everyone who embraced *Easy Beans*, cooked their way through it and kept asking when the second book was going to be written.

To family and friends who once again gamely tasted and tested every variety of bean dish.

To Val Spiedel, our innovative cover designer, for her artistic integrity.

To Neil Thacker, cartoonist, for once again making beans fun loving, lighthearted characters.

To Moira Chicilo, for her valuable contribution to the editorial and layout process.

To our new distributors for saying those magic words, "Yes, this will sell."

And special thanks to George Trim of North Star Publications, a role model for all mentors.

Why We Did It Again

What a dramatic change in the world of beans since our first book, *Easy Beans*, was published in 1994. Because of continuing research and an information explosion, there is now more emphasis on legumes as an important food source. A desire by North Americans to eat healthier by cutting fat, not flavor, has sparked an even wider interest in bean cuisine.

But why another bean cookbook? The simple answer is we love to cook with beans, peas and lentils and still had some great recipes to share. Spurred on by the positive feedback about *Easy Beans*, we continued to experiment, combining more types of beans with an even wider range of ingredients. Before we knew it we had the makings of another book!

Like our first bean book, *More Easy Beans* maintains the same, simple layout and keeps the emphasis on 'easy'. We have however added some new twists:
- the selection of beans have been expanded to include romano, adzuki and mung beans
- we have partnered beans with such interesting foods as orzo, gorgonzola and asiago cheese
- 'kid-friendly' bean recipes have been included so that healthy eating can start at a young age

It's been fun; it's been a brain stretcher. Thanks for encouraging us to continue writing. We hope you enjoy the recipes in *More Easy Beans* as much as you did in *Easy Beans*.

Beans are Best

The Asian Food Pyramid

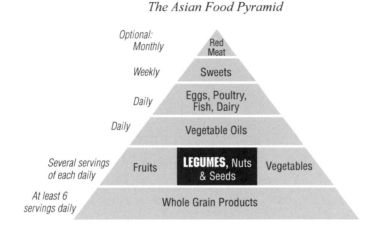

Optional: Monthly — Red Meat

Weekly — Sweets

Daily — Eggs, Poultry, Fish, Dairy

Daily — Vegetable Oils

Several servings of each daily — Fruits, **LEGUMES, Nuts & Seeds**, Vegetables

At least 6 servings daily — Whole Grain Products

The Mediterranean Food Pyramid

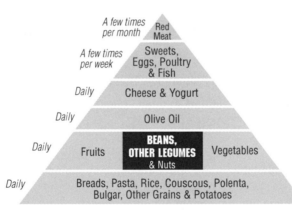

A few times per month — Red Meat

A few times per week — Sweets, Eggs, Poultry & Fish

Daily — Cheese & Yogurt

Daily — Olive Oil

Daily — Fruits, **BEANS, OTHER LEGUMES & Nuts**, Vegetables

Daily — Breads, Pasta, Rice, Couscous, Polenta, Bulgar, Other Grains & Potatoes

Two new food pyramids, the Asian and Mediterranean, are the latest trend in educated eating and are helping legumes (beans, peas and lentils) gain the recognition they deserve in North America.

These two pyramids follow in the wake of the U.S. Department of Agriculture "diet pyramid" in 1992, where beans were included in a food group with other proteins such as meat, poultry and fish. The Harvard School of Public Health and the World Health Organization then developed the Mediterranean and Asian pyramids (Cornell University also worked on the Asian Pyramid one).

The Mediterranean Food Pyramid recommends daily servings of grains, LEGUMES, fruit, vegetables, cheese and yogurt. Meat, poultry and fish are served less frequently.

The Asian Pyramid indicates a radical change in a healthy eating program where grains, fruit, LEGUMES and vegetables become the mainstay of any diet and meat and dairy products become optional.

Both the Mediterranean and the Asian Food Diet recommend eating more foods containing plant proteins. Both also encourage more frequent servings of carbohydrates and vegetables. The major difference is that in the Asian Diet less fat is consumed.

We do not know the exact relationship between diet and disease but it has become accepted that healthy eating can improve our chances of preventing diseases such as heart disease, strokes and some forms of cancer.

LEGUMES provide a healthy food choice because they are:

Low in Fat

■ The new food guides suggest we choose lower fat foods more often.

■ Fats can either be saturated or unsaturated. Saturated fat tends to raise blood cholesterol levels. Unsaturated fat is the "good guy" and helps lower blood cholesterol.

■ Beans (except soy beans) contain only about four percent fat, all of which is unsaturated. For example, one cup (250 mL) of white beans, kidney beans or lentils contain only one gram of fat.

■ There have been studies which show that women who eat less fat have less breast cancer.

High in Protein

■ The new food pyramids are encouraging us to increase the amount of vegetable protein in our diet.

■ Legumes have the highest concentration of vegetable protein of any food.

■ In China and Japan they consume 85 to 90 percent of their protein from vegetarian sources.

■ Research is showing that plant protein helps protect the heart by lowering blood cholesterol levels in most people.

■ The vegetable protein in beans is not complete, but when beans are combined with grains, seeds or nuts they make a complete protein.

■ Beans, combined with grains, are a prime source of protein in many countries and have been for centuries.

High in Fibre

There are two kinds of fibre:

- Soluble fibre:
    - a sticky, gel-like water soluble fibre.
    - in almost all foods only 1/4 of the fibre is soluble.
    - one serving of beans can meet 1/2 the daily requirement.
    - helps to lower cholesterol in most people.
    - helps to combat heart disease and may help prevent colon cancer.
- Insoluble fibre:
    - once called roughage, insoluble fibre improves regularity.

Loaded with Complex Carbohydrates

- Complex carbohydrates are foods containing fibre and starch. Carbohydrates are the body's best source of energy and should supply half our daily energy needs (calories to most of us).
- Foods rich in carbohydrates are thought to increase metabolism and speed the burning of calories.
- Goods sources of complex carbohydrates are beans, peas and lentils, whole grain breads and cereals, fruits and vegetables.

Rich in Minerals and Vitamins

- Minerals:
    - high in potassium and phosphorus
    - moderate amounts of calcium and iron
    - contain magnesium and zinc
- Vitamins:
    - contain the B vitamins except B12
    - rich in folic acid which is important for pregnant women by helping to prevent neural birth defects such as spina bifida.
    - may help protect against cervical cancer.

Other Bean Benefits

- One of the least allergenic foods.
- Gluten free – a good way to add variety to gluten free diets.
- Good for diabetics – both complex carbohydrates and fibre help keep blood sugar on an even keel.

Discovering Bean Varieties

White Beans

■ **Navy** - a small, white, oval bean. A staple in North American pantries for years. Extremely versatile, from the classic Boston Baked Beans to upscale salads.

■ **Great Northern** - the bigger brother of the navy bean but slightly larger and whiter. It is a interchangeable with the navy bean.

■ **White Kidney** - same shape as the familiar red kidney, only white. It is a common substitute in Italian recipes when cannellini beans are called for.

Red Beans

■ **Red Kidney** - as familiar as the navy, especially canned. This bean is dark red and kidney shaped as the name suggests. Commonly used for chili but now appearing in salads and soups.

■ **Small Red or Mexican** - often called by either name. It is smaller than the kidney, a richer red and has an oval shape. Because of its size, it is a less dominant substitute for the kidney and pinto bean.

■ **Pinto** - a pinkish brown speckled bean traditionally a staple of Hispanic cooking. Now widely used because it combines so tastily with a variety of seasonings. Use in place of red kidney or small red Mexican bean.

■ **Romano** - also called the borlotto or cranberry bean. It is a mottled pink and light brown colour, about 1/2" (0.5 cm) long. After soaking and cooking, the color changes to a uniform dark beige. Important in Italian cuisine.

- **Adzuki** - also spelled adsuki, aduki. A small, round, dark reddish brown bean important in Japanese and Chinese cooking. It has a creamy yellow interior. The texture is soft; the taste is sweet and nutty.

Black Beans
- **Black or Turtle Beans** - black, small, oval beans with a glossy coat. Adaptable for every aspect of cooking. *(Special note:* fermented black beans are black soy beans and have no relation to these beans.)

...And There's More
- **Black-Eyed Peas** - cream colored bean with a black spot in the middle. A favorite in southern U.S. cooking; they do not have to be soaked.

- **Chick Peas or Garbanzo** - the same bean with an interchangeable name. Looks like a tan, rough skinned nut. It has an irregular round shape.

- **Lima Beans** - canned and frozen, they are a lovely soft green color. In the dried form, they come in two sizes and are white. The texture is mealy.

- **Mung Beans -** very small, round and olive green. They are most commonly used for sprouting – either do-it-yourself or find in the produce section. No soaking required.

Lentils and Split Peas
- **Green/Brown** - labelled green or brown, they are all the same lentil. Small, flattened discs that have a dusty, rather than glossy, look.

- **Red** - actually more a bright orange. Can be used instead of the green/brown ones. The result is a soup that is slightly lighter in color.

- **Split Peas** - both green and yellow. Instantly recognizable and a national favorite in soup.

Buying Legumes
- **Dried** - in bulk or prepackaged.
- **Canned** - cooked and ready to use. Be sure to drain and rinse well.
- **Frozen** - ready to use. The plus is that no sodium is added.
- **Dehydrated** - mostly available for instant soups and for refried beans.

Where to Find Them
- **Supermarkets** - in the bulk food department
  - in the frozen food section
  - with the other canned vegetables
  - in the specialty areas (e.g., Mexican, East Indian)

- **Natural Food Stores** - in bulk or canned organic
- **Health and Bulk Food Stores**
- **Specialty Shops** - gourmet packaging (e.g., spices are added to soup mixes and packaged as gifts)
- **Ethnic Shops** - e.g., Mexican, Greek, East Indian

Useful Hints
It is almost impossible to tell the age of dry beans in the bin unless they are obviously shrivelled or cracked. Shop in a popular spot where the turnover is high. Build a rapport with the owner or manager and ask how long the beans have been there. If you try cooking beans that won't soften, take them back and complain. Beans are still suffering the reputation of being difficult to cook with simply because the supply was not fresh.

Canned & Frozen Beans & Lentils
Have every variety in your cupboard for instant meals. Try different brands as some are obviously superior - firm, no burst skins. However, don't rely on cans for salads, except for chick peas. You can hit a very soft batch just as company is arriving. All varieties of frozen beans are now finding a place on the shelves.

Soaking & Cooking Dried Beans

What to Soak

Dried beans and whole peas must be soaked before cooking. You do not have to soak split peas, lentils, black-eyed peas or mung beans. However, they should be rinsed before cooking.

There are two soaking methods:

The Quick Soak Method

- Sort through the beans, discarding the broken and shrivelled ones.
- Rinse beans under cold running water. A colander is useful for this step.
- Place beans in large saucepan and cover with three times the volume of water (for 1 cup (250 mL) beans, use 3 cups (750 mL) of water).
- Bring to boil. Simmer gently for 2-3 minutes. Remove from heat and let stand for at least one hour.
- Drain beans and rinse under cold running water. Store covered in the refrigerator or freezer if not using immediately.

The Slow Soak Method

- As in the quick soak method, sort and wash beans.
- Place beans in a large bowl. Cover with three times as much fresh cold water as beans (for 1 cup (250 mL) beans, use 3 cups (750 mL) of water).
- Let sit for at least four hours or overnight in a cool place.
- Drain beans and rinse. Refrigerate, covered, if not using immediately.

After Soaking

■ If not used immediately, soaked legumes can be stored, covered, in the refrigerator for up to three days.

■ Freeze for future use. When frozen, cooked and soaked beans look very muck alike. The authors must confess that we have tossed a salad with soaked beans. You only do it once! Our recommendation is to freeze them after cooking.

Cooking Chart

Soaked Beans:	Cooking Time:
Navy	35-40 minutes
Great Northern	40-45 minutes
Pinto	30-35 minutes
Kidney, red or white	35-40 minutes
Black	30-35 minutes
Lima	55-60 minutes
Chick Pea (garbanzo)	80 minutes
Small Red	30-35 minutes
Romano	40-45 minutes
Adzuki	20-25 minutes
Unsoaked Beans:	**Cooking Time:**
Black-Eyed Peas	30 minutes
Lentils & Split Peas	20-25 minutes
Mung	15-20 minutes

Cooking Method

■ Place the soaked beans in a large saucepan. Cover with at least 3" (7.5 cm) of cold water. Bring to boil. Reduce heat, cover and simmer gently according to chart. Do not boil as skins might burst. Drain and rinse.

■ Test for doneness by biting. Try at least five beans from the middle of the pot. They should be tender but firm and have no taste of starchiness.

■ To prevent foaming, add 1 Tbsp (15 mL) of vegetable oil to the cooking water.

Tips

- Add acid foods such as tomato juice, wine or vinegar in the last stages of cooking.
- Microwaves are not a time saver when cooking beans. Handy for heating canned beans and leftovers.
- Cook at least double the amount you need. Freeze the rest for quick use later.

Helpful Information

If your beans aren't tender by the chart times, the reason could be:

- *Old beans.* Try a more popular market.
- *The altitude.* The higher you are the longer it takes.
- *Hard water.* Just keep cooking and "bite" testing.

Yields

Most Beans:

1 cup (250 mL) dried = 2 1/4 - 2 1/2 cups (550 -625 mL) cooked

Exception:

Chick peas (garbanzos), lima beans and Great Northern beans yield even more:

1 cup (250 mL) dried = 2 1/2 - 3 cups (625-796 mL) cooked

Canned Equivalents:

14 oz (398 mL) = 1 1/2 cups (375 mL)

10 oz (540 mL) = 2 1/4 cups (540 mL)

28 oz (796 mL) = 3 - 3 1/4 cups (750- 796 mL)

Exact amounts are not important in bean cooking. Just add a little liquid if the dish looks dry.

Storing

- Dried beans, peas and lentils should be kept in the cupboard in a moisture-proof lidded container. Try to use within six months.
- Soaked or cooked legumes stay fresh for a maximum of three days in the refrigerator. Store in a covered container.
- Freeze beans in portions suitable for the recipes you use. Labelled ziploc bags and plastic cottage cheese containers, etc., are handy. Be sure to label the kind of bean it is as well if it is soaked or cooked.

Bean Companions

We are repeating our cupboard checklist from *Easy Beans*, with a few interesting additions. We are assuming that your cupboard includes such herbs as basil, oregano and thyme, and spices such as chili powder and paprika. Other bean companions are listed below.

Dried Herbs & Spices

- **Bay Leaves** - a must. Add to beans while simmering. Remove before serving!
- **Cajun Seasoning** - a large variable blend of peppers and spices. Used in southern cooking.
- **Coriander** - comes ground or whole. Actually dried cilantro seeds but don't substitute for fresh cilantro -- it has a very different taste.
- **Cumin** *(ground)* - another must. A spice used in many Mexican and Middle Eastern recipes. Works well with chili powder.
- **Curry Powder** - a blend of spices common in Indian dishes. Buy a good brand, preferably East Indian.
- **Fine Herbs** - a combination of basil, thyme, rosemary, dill weed, savory, marjoram and parsley. Great when you can't decide what to use. Get seven for the price of one!
- **Italian Seasoning** - another combination containing oregano, basil, thyme, rosemary, sage and savory.
- **Garlic** - fresh is best but when in a hurry you can use garlic powder or processed minced garlic in jars.
- **Red Pepper Flakes** - add fire to any dish. Remember, a little goes a long way.
- **Rosemary** - works well with white beans and chick peas (garbanzo beans). Combines well with oregano and thyme.
- **Savory** - called the bean herb because it mates happily with all of them. Add to the beans while simmering.
- **Turmeric** - an inexpensive substitute for saffron. It gives a pungent taste and a yellow color to dishes.

Fresh Herbs

Use fresh herbs whenever possible. Look for them in the specialty area of the vegetable department. In the summer you might try growing your own. In cooking, the rule is use three times as much fresh to dried. For example, 3 Tbsp (45 mL) to 1 Tbsp (15 mL) dried.

Other Friends Are

- **Cheeses** - many cheeses such as feta, Monterey Jack and cheddar combine well with beans. In the exotic category are asiago and gorgonzola. These Italian cheeses are expensive but delicious. A little goes a long way.

- **Chilies** - we use small canned diced green chilies for convenience. Often called for in Southwestern and Mexican recipes.

- **Chipotle Peppers** - are jalapeno peppers ripened and smoked. They are extremely hot. Usually canned in adobo sauce (a tomato sauce). Found in the Mexican section of your supermarket or in specialty food stores.

- **Dijon Mustard** - this French mustard has won us over.

- **Grains** - bulgar and couscous are used in Middle Eastern cooking and available prepackaged in the specialty section of supermarkets. Also can be purchased in bulk.

- **Hot Pepper Sauce** - Tabasco sauce is the most common brand and may be used in place of jalapeno peppers.

- **Jalapeno Peppers** - buy fresh from the specialty area of vegetable departments. Watch out -- they can be hot!

- **Olive Oil** - choose a good quality extra virgin olive oil; you will notice the difference.

- **Salsa** - a spicy tomato dip or sauce used to enliven some Mexican recipes.

- **Soy Sauce** - used in Oriental cooking. Now available in 'lite' varieties with reduced salt.

- **Stock** - (vegetable, chicken or beef). If you don't have time to make your own stock (recipe page 56), use good quality bouillon cubes or instant granules.

- **Vegetable Oil** - Canola, sunflower or safflower are good choices.

- **Grapeseed Oil** - watch for this one -- it's new!

- **Vinegars** - balsamic, red wine, white wine, cider vinegars, all complement beans. They keep well so stock up.

No Problem

"Well, I'd really like to start including beans in my diet, but..." This is a comment we sometimes hear when we talk to potential bean enthusiasts. Here are some suggestions to bridge any bean eating barrier you might have.

But first, what exactly is going on with legumes and our digestive systems? Simply put, the reason for gas after eating beans (and cabbage, broccoli and some fruits) is this:
  - complex sugars are not broken down in the upper intestine.
  - these sugars pass intact into the lower intestine where they are metabolized (broken down) into simple sugars by bacteria. The by-product is perfectly normal gas.

To smooth the digestive process, bean cooks try the following:

■ **Tolerance** - the more beans you eat, the less trouble you will have with them. Slip into the bean world twice a week with recipes that do not have beans as the main ingredient (Pesto Fettucine with Beans, Spinach White Bean Salad, for example).

■ **Preparation** - proper cooking is important. After soaking the beans, discard the water and rinse well. Cook in fresh water, discard that water and rinse again. Test at least five cooked beans to make sure there is no starchy taste left. Always drain and rinse canned beans.

■ **Beano** - a commercial product found mainly in drugstores, health and natural food stores. It is now a tablet to be taken before meals as well as in liquid enzyme form.

■ **Kombu** - a sea vegetable that appears to have properties which help soften beans. Add a 4" strip to the cooking water after the soak stage.

■ **Epazote** - Hispanic cooks recommend the addition of this weedlike herb to the cooking water. It looks like dried cilantro with a tough stalk. Not so easy to find but ask in specialty food stores.

■ **Ginger** - a staple in East Indian cuisine both for the flavor and its digestive help. Again, add fresh or dried at the cooking stage.

■ **Freezing** - we're still being told that it helps to freeze the beans after the soak stage. It's worth a try, but just remember to label the container 'soaked' and save your teeth a surprise.

Starters

Starters

Creamy Frijole Dip

In Spanish, the word for bean is frijole (free-ho-lee). We don't know the word for 'smooth' but that is what this dip is. Partner with tortilla strips (recipe below) for a different presentation.

1	can (19 oz/540 mL) black beans,* drained and rinsed	1
1	pkg (8 oz/ 250 g) spreadable low fat cream cheese	1
3 ´	cloves garlic, minced	3
1 Tbsp	chili powder	15 mL
	juice of 1 lime	
	grated rind of 1 lime	
	tortilla strips for dipping (recipe follows)	

* If using dried beans, soak and cook 3/4 cup (175 mL) according to directions an pages 10 and 11.

■ Place all ingredients in a food processor or blender and blend until smooth.

■ Serve at room temperature in a small bowl, garnish with any or all of the following: sour cream, grated cheese or chopped green onions. Keeps well in refrigerator.

Makes 2 cups (500 mL).

To make tortilla strips:

■ Cut 8" (20 cm) or 10" (25 cm) flour tortilla rounds in strips 1/2" (1 cm) wide. Cut middle strips of tortilla in half.

■ Place on ungreased cookie sheet. Bake at 350⁰F (180⁰C) for 8-10 minutes, turning once.

■ They look best served upright in a tall stemmed glass.

Uncle Bobino's Salsa

One of Uncle Bobino's frequent trips to Mexico resulted in him finding this zingy salsa. The special flavors are the chipotle (chee-poe-tlay) and roasted peppers. Treat yourself to a can of chipotle peppers in adobo sauce as you'll be seeing them in more and more recipes. We use them in two other appetizers – Pinto Bean Dip and Spicy Bean Dip. They also add a kick to the Mexican Baked Beans in the Main Dishes section.

3	large ripe tomatoes, peeled, seeded and diced	3
1/2 cup	green onions, chopped	125 mL
1 cup	cooked kernel corn	250 mL
1 cup	cooked black beans*	250 mL
1/2 cup	chopped cilantro	125 mL
1	roasted red pepper**, chopped	1
2 tsp	canned chipotle peppers in adobo sauce, finely minced	10 mL
1 tsp	lime juice (fresh if possible)	5 mL
2	cloves garlic, minced	2
1 tsp	salt	5 mL

* If using dried beans, soak and cook 1/2 cup (125 mL) according to directions on pages 10 and 11.
** See directions for roasting peppers on page 38.

- In large bowl, mix all ingredients together.
- Let stand at least one hour.
- Serve with tortilla chips for dipping.

Yields 2 1/2 cups (625 mL).

Pesto Garbanzo Dip

This simple recipe has been tested with many of the different pesto sauces on the market. Fortunately for the "time challenged", all were equally satisfactory.

1 cup	prepared pesto sauce	250 mL
1	can (19 oz/540 mL) chick peas, (garbanzo beans) drained and rinsed	1

- Place the 2 ingredients in a food processor or blender. Whirl until smooth. If the dip is a little stiff, add 2 Tbsp (25 mL) of warm water.
- Store in refrigerator until an hour before serving. Serve with carrot and celery sticks.
- Can keep in refrigerator for 5 days. Freezes well.

Makes 1 1/2 cups (375 mL).

Pinto Bean Dip

Chipotle peppers are what make this dip unusual. They are ripened and smoked jalapeno peppers with a bite. You will find them in small cans in the Mexican section of your supermarket or in specialty food stores. After you have opened the can, store remaining peppers in a tightly lidded jar in the refrigerator.

1 cup	cooked pinto beans*	250 mL
1	clove garlic, minced	1
1/4	green pepper, chopped	1/4
2 Tbsp	tomato paste	25 mL
2 Tbsp	cider vinegar	25 mL
2 Tbsp	water	25 mL
1 tsp	canned chipotle peppers in adobo sauce**	5 mL
1/4 tsp	paprika	1 mL
1/4 tsp	chili powder	1 mL

* If using dried beans soak and cook 1/2 cup (125 mL) according to directions on pages 10 and 11.
** Start with 1 tsp (5 mL) and add more if you like it hotter.

■ In food processor or blender, place all ingredients. Blend until smooth.

■ Serve with warm pita bread or as a dip for raw vegetables.

Makes 1 cup (250 mL).

White Bean Canapés

What better combination than artichoke hearts and sundried tomatoes? These easy-to-make canapés will be sure to please.

1 cup	cooked navy beans*	250 mL
1	green onion, chopped	1
1	clove garlic, minced	1
1/3 cup	artichoke hearts, finely chopped	75 mL
8	sundried tomatoes, finely chopped	8
2 Tbsp	chopped fresh basil	25 mL
1 tsp	olive oil	5 mL
1 tsp	lemon juice	5 mL
	freshly grated parmesan cheese	
1	French baguette, cut in 1/2" (1 cm) slices	1

* If using dried beans, soak and cook 1/2 cup (125 mL) according to directions on pages 10 and 11.

- In a food processor or blender, place beans, onion and garlic. Blend until smooth.
- Remove mixture to a small bowl and gently stir in other ingredients. Mixture will not be smooth.
- Spread white bean mixture on baguette slices. Top with parmesan cheese. Place on baking sheet.
- Bake in 400°F (200°C) oven for 4 minutes or until mixture is thoroughly heated.

Yields approximately 30.

Peanut Butter Hummus

No problem with the ingredients for this dip. Peanut butter, a North American comfort food, replaces the tahini of a traditional hummus. Guaranteed kids as well as adults will love it.

1	can (19 oz/540 mL) chick peas (garbanzo beans), drained and rinsed	1
2 Tbsp	water	25 mL
1/4 cup	lemon juice	50 mL
1/4 cup	olive oil	50 mL
1/4 cup	peanut butter	50 mL
3 Tbsp	chopped parsley	45 mL
3	cloves garlic, minced	3
1	bay leaf, crushed	1
1/2 tsp	salt	3 mL

■ In food processor or blender, place all ingredients. Blend until smooth.

■ Serve with warm pita bread or raw vegetables.

Makes 2 1/2 cups (625 mL).

Spicy Black Bean Dip

This dip has been an instant winner with everyone. Don't be frightened off by the long list of ingredients. It is quickly prepared and just as quickly eaten. The chipotle peppers are a necessary ingredient and, with their winning flavor, are sure to become a North American cupboard staple. Look for them in the Mexican section of your supermarket or a specialty food store.

2 cups	cooked black beans*	500 mL
1	roasted red pepper**	1
2 Tbsp	canned diced green chilies	25 mL
3 Tbsp	chopped onions	45 mL
1/4 cup	tomato paste	50 mL
1/4 cup	white vinegar	50 mL
2 Tbsp	lime juice	25 mL
2	garlic cloves, minced	2
1 tsp	ground cumin	5 mL
1 tsp	ground coriander	5 mL
1 tsp	chili powder	5 mL
1/2 tsp	salt	3 mL
2 tsp	canned chipotle peppers in adobo sauce	10 mL

* If using dried beans, soak and cook 3/4 cup (175 mL) according to directions on pages 10 and 11.
** See directions on page 38.

■ In food processor, combine all ingredients except black beans. Blend until smooth.

■ Gradually add black beans and purée until smooth.

■ Present dip garnished with a cilantro sprig in a glass or pottery bowl. Serve with tortilla chips or raw vegetables.

Make 2 cups (500 mL).

Crostini with Beans

We have all eagerly embraced Tuscany cuisine. Crostini is a toasted slice of Italian or French bread with a topping. Some tasty toppings are liver pate, a black olive purée, or the popular bruschetta. Naturally we lean toward this delicious white kidney bean crostini. Use canned beans - they are soft and cook quickly.

1 Tbsp	olive oil	15 mL
4	garlic cloves, minced	4
1	can (19 oz/540 mL) white kidney beans, drained and rinsed	1
1/3 cup	water	75 mL
1 tsp	dried basil	5 mL
1/8 tsp	freshly ground pepper	1 mL
1	French baguette, cut in 1/2" (1 cm) slices, toasted	1

- In medium saucepan, sauté garlic in oil over medium heat for 2 minutes.
- Add beans, water and seasonings. Cook and stir often for 10 minutes or until mixture thickens. Lightly mash the beans leaving about 1/2 of them whole.

To serve cold:

- Top toasted baguette slices with 1 heaping teaspoon of bean mixture. Garnish with diced tomatoes or a sprig of fresh basil.

To serve warm:

- Top freshly toasted baguette slice with hot bean mixture. Garnish with a piece of sundried tomato or diced fresh tomatoes.
- Or, make crostini ahead. Just before serving, heat in microwave for 10 to 20 seconds.

Makes approximately 20 crostinis.

Mini Nachos

Just as tasty and popular with guests as a heaping plateful of nachos, these single, bite size morsels are easy to prepare. There is one downside; they CANNOT be made too far ahead because the beans and tomato make the chips soft. Canned refried black beans are available in the Mexican section of your market or make your own (recipe on page 109).

1	package round tortilla chips	1
1/2 cup	refried black beans*	125 mL
2	tomatoes, pulp removed, finely diced	2
1	jalapeno pepper, finely diced**	1
3/4 cup	Monterey Jack or cheddar cheese, shredded	175 mL

* Use canned or recipe on page 109.
** If you like it hot, use 2.

■ In small bowl, mix diced tomato and pepper together.

■ Spread each tortilla chip with refried beans.

■ Heap a scant teaspoon of tomato mixture on beans.

■ Top with shredded cheese.

■ Bake in oven at 350⁰F (180⁰C) for 10 minutes. Serve immediately.

Makes 20 mini nachos.

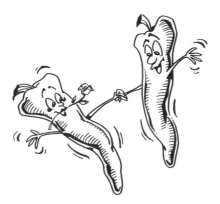

Split Pea & Walnut Purée

Yellow split peas have finally been given a chance to appear in other places besides soup. The curry and yogurt give this dip an exotic touch.

3/4 cup	dried yellow split peas	175 mL
1/3 cup	walnuts	75 mL
1/3 cup	low fat yogurt	75 mL
1 Tbsp	lemon juice	15 mL
1 Tbsp	olive oil	15 mL
2	green onions	2
1	clove garlic, minced	1
1 tsp	curry powder	5 mL

■ Rinse and drain split peas. Place in saucepan and cover with 3" (7.5 cm) of water. Bring to boil and reduce heat. Cover and cook for 25 minutes. Drain and rinse.

■ In food processor, combine all ingredients. Purée until smooth.

■ Place in a colorful ceramic bowl. Decorate with sprigs of cilantro or parsley. Serve with carrot sticks.

Makes 1 1/2 cups (375 mL).

Black Bean Tarts

Plan on only 1 or 2 of these hearty appetizers per person. The dollop of lime sour cream is a light finishing touch.

3 cups	cooked black beans*	750 mL
1	10 oz (300 gm) package frozen corn	1
1	red pepper, finely chopped	1
1/2 cup	chopped cilantro	125 mL
1 1/2 cups	grated Monterey Jack cheese	375 mL
2	jalapeno peppers, seeded and finely chopped	2
2	green onions, finely chopped	2
1 1/2 tsp	ground cumin	8 mL
1 1/2 tsp	chili powder	8 mL
	packaged unbaked tart shells	
Lime Sour Cream:		
1/2 cup	sour cream	125 mL
1 tsp	lime juice, or to taste	5 mL

* If using dried beans, soak and cook 1 1/4 cups (300 mL) according to directions on pages 10 and 11.

- Purée 1 cup (250 mL) of the cooked black beans.
- Cook corn as directed.
- Combine puréed black beans, rest of the beans, and remaining ingredients. Gently stir.
- Spoon into tart shells and bake in a 350°F (180°C) oven for 15 to 20 minutes.
- Serve, topped with lime sour cream.

Makes 24 to 48, depending on tart shell size.

Layered Mexican Appetizer

Some like it hot - some like it cold – tasty either way but be warned that when it's hot it's a bit runny. You can use low fat sour cream for the cold version but splurge on the real thing if serving it warm.

1	can (14 oz/398 mL) refried black beans *	1
1 cup	sour cream	250 mL
1	jalapeno pepper, finely chopped **	1
1/2 cup	sliced pitted black olives (optional)	125 mL
1 cup	seeded, diced, unpeeled tomatoes	250 mL
4	green onions, chopped	4
1/2 cup	grated cheddar cheese	125 mL
	tortilla chips	

* Can use 1 1/2 cups (375 mL) black refried beans (see page 109).
** Can use 1 Tbsp (15 mL) of canned diced jalapeno peppers.

- *First Layer:* In a 9 inch (23 cm) oven proof pie plate, spread the refried beans.
- *Second Layer:* Add jalapeno peppers to sour cream and spread over beans.
- *Third Layer:* Layer with black olives.
- *Fourth Layer:* Combine tomatoes and green onions and spread on olives.
- Sprinkle cheese on top.
- Serve with tortilla chips for dipping.

If serving hot:

- Heat at 350°F (180°C) for 15-20 minutes or until mixture is bubbly and cheese is melted. Let stand for 10 to 15 minutes.

Serves 8-10.

Soups

Soups

Black Bean Orzo Soup

*This soup has been tested many times using canned tomatoes, fresh tomatoes, tomato juice and leaving the tomatoes out entirely. Our testers came to a consensus and rated the juice the highest. For 5 more black bean soup recipes consult our first book, **Easy Beans**. Orzo is a pasta that looks like rice.*

2 Tbsp	vegetable oil	25 mL
1	medium onion, chopped	1
2	cloves garlic, minced	2
1	red pepper, finely chopped	1
4 cups	vegetable stock*	1 L
1/2 cup	orzo	125 mL
2 cups	cooked black beans**	500 mL
1 cup	tomato juice	250 mL
1 tsp	dried thyme	5 mL
1 tsp	dried rosemary	5 mL
	salt and pepper to taste	

* Can use bouillon cubes or granules. Follow package instructions. Recipe for vegetable stock on page 56.
** If using dried beans, soak and cook 3/4 cup (175 mL) according to directions on pages 10 and 11.

- In soup pot, sauté onion, garlic and pepper in oil over medium heat for 3 minutes.
- Add vegetable stock and orzo. Simmer, covered, for 10 minutes.
- Add remaining ingredients and simmer 20 minutes.
- Taste and adjust seasonings if necessary. Add more juice if soup is too thick.

Serves 4-6.

Mung Bean Chowder

Bok choy, a major ingredient of this soup, is a Chinese green with a delicate, sweet flavor. It is typically used in a stir-fry but we decided it would make an unusual addition to this soup.

1/2 cup	dried mung beans	125 mL
2 tsp	vegetable oil	10 ml
1/2 cup	finely chopped onion	125 ml
2 Tbsp	sesame seeds	25 mL
1/3 cup	uncooked rice*	75 mL
6 cups	vegetable stock**	1.5 L
1/4 cup	chopped parsley	50 mL
2 Tbsp	soy sauce	25 mL
1/2 tsp	ground ginger	3 mL
1/2 tsp	dry mustard	3 mL
1	bunch bok choy, chopped	1

* If you use brown rice you will need to cook the soup an additional 20 minutes.
** Can use bouillon cubes or instant granules. Follow package instructions.
Recipe for vegetable stock on page 56.

■ Rinse mung beans. Bring 3 cups (750 mL) water to the boil. Add mung beans, removed from heat. Let stand 15 minutes. Drain and rinse.

■ While beans are soaking, in a large saucepan, sauté onions in oil over medium heat for 3 minutes.

■ Add sesame seeds and rice. Sauté 5 minutes more. Add vegetable stock.

■ Add drained beans to soup mixture. Bring to boil. Reduce heat. Cover and simmer for 20 minutes.

■ Add remaining ingredients and simmer 5 minutes more.

Serves 6.

Lentil Mung Bean Soup

Super fast because the mung beans soak for only 15 minutes while you sauté the vegetables. Lentils, of course, need no soaking. Mung beans are commonly used for sprouting but their earthy flavor is gaining them wider popularity.

1/2 cup	dried mung beans	125 mL
1 Tbsp	vegetable oil	15 mL
1	medium onion, chopped	1
3	stalks celery, chopped	3
2	medium carrots, chopped	2
6 cups	vegetable stock*	1.5 L
1/2 cup	dried green/brown lentils	125 mL
2 tsp	ground cumin	10 mL
1 tsp	turmeric	5 mL
1 tsp	coriander	5 mL
1/2 tsp	chili powder	3 mL
1/2 tsp	salt	3 mL

* Can use bouillon cubes or instant granules. Follow package directions. Recipe for vegetable stock on page 56.

■ Rinse mung beans. Bring 3 cups (750 mL) water to the boil. Add mung beans, remove from heat. Let stand 15 minutes. Drain and rinse.

■ In soup pot, sauté onion, celery and carrots in oil over medium heat for 5 minutes.

■ Rinse lentils. Add lentils, drained mung beans and stock to vegetables. Bring to boil, reduce heat, cover and simmer for 45 minutes.

■ Add spices and simmer 15 minutes more.

Serves 6.

Split Pea & Mint Soup

Not just a soup for the summer now that fresh mint is widely available in the produce department. A nice surprise for anyone who thinks they know exactly what split pea soup tastes like.

1 Tbsp	olive oil	15 mL
1	leek (white part plus 1/3 the green), chopped	1
2	carrots, chopped	2
2	stalks celery, chopped	2
5 cups	vegetable stock*	1.25 L
1 cup	dried split green peas, rinsed	250 mL
2 Tbsp	chopped fresh mint	25 mL
2 tsp	Dijon mustard	10 mL
1/4 cup	low fat yogurt	50 mL

* Can use instant boullion cubes or granules, if desired. Recipe for vegetable stock on page 56.

■ In large saucepan, sauté vegetables in oil over medium heat for 5 minutes.

■ Add vegetable stock and split peas. Bring to boil. Reduce heat. Cover and simmer for 25 minutes.

■ Add mint and mustard and simmer 10 minutes more.

■ Serve in bowls topped with a dollop of yogurt.

Serves 4.

Pumpkin Soup

At last the wonderful pumpkin has managed to be noticed all year round. Until recently only seen as a carved face or a bakery item, it is now a featured soup or vegetable in many upscale restaurants.

1 Tbsp	vegetable oil	15 mL
1	small onion, chopped	1
1	garlic clove, minced	1
6 cups	vegetable stock*	1.5 L
1 cup	split yellow peas, rinsed	250 mL
1 cup	canned pumpkin**	250 mL
2 Tbsp	honey	25 mL
1/2 tsp	ground nutmeg	3 mL
	light sour cream	

* Can use boullion cubes or instant granules. Follow package directions. Recipe for vegetable stock on page 56.
** Do not use pumpkin pie filling!

■ In large saucepan, sauté onion and garlic in oil over medium heat for 5 minutes.

■ Add remaining ingredients except sour cream. Bring to boil and reduce heat. Cover and simmer for 35 minutes, or until split peas are soft. Remove from heat.

■ Purée in food processor until soup is smooth.

■ Return to saucepan. Reheat.

■ Serve in individual bowls with a dollop of light sour cream on top.

Serves 6.

Cilantro Split Pea Soup

The answer to, "What's that mysterious flavor in this soup?", is Dijon mustard. Because the split peas need no soaking, this is a 40 minute dish, from in-the-pot to on-the-table.

1 cup	dried yellow split peas	250 mL
6 cups	vegetable stock*	1.5 L
2 Tbsp	olive oil	25 mL
2	medium onions, finely chopped	2
6	medium carrots, finely chopped	6
2 Tbsp	Dijon mustard	25 mL
1/4 cup	finely chopped cilantro	50 mL
1/2 tsp	salt	2 mL
	freshly ground pepper to taste	

* Can use bouillon cubes or instant granules if desired. Recipe for vegetable stock on page 56.

■ Rinse split peas.

■ In saucepan, combine peas and vegetable stock. Bring to boil and reduce heat. Cover and simmer for 20 minutes.

■ While peas are cooking, heat olive oil and sauté onions and carrots for 5 minutes.

■ Add to yellow peas and simmer 15 minutes more.

■ Add mustard, cilantro, salt and pepper and simmer an additional 5 minutes.

Serves 6.

Black-Eyed Pea Soup

Some of the comments about this colorful soup from our testers were "fantastic", and "excellent". One suggested that you could use less liquid and have a great chili. Just one more example of the flexibility of beans!

2 Tbsp	vegetable oil	25 mL
2	stalks celery, chopped	2
1	medium onion, chopped	1
1	green pepper, chopped	1
2	cloves garlic, minced	2
1 cup	dried black-eyed peas	250 mL
1	can (28oz/796mL) diced tomatoes	1
3 cups	vegetable stock*	750 mL
2 Tbsp	chili powder	25 mL
1 1/2 tsp	each: oregano and basil	8 mL
3	bay leaves	3
1 tsp	salt	5 mL
1 1/2 cups	fresh spinach, washed and cut in 1" (2.5 cm) strips	375 mL
	freshly ground pepper	

* Can use bouillion cubes or granules if desired. Follow package instructions. Recipe for vegetable stock on page 56.

■ In soup pot, sauté celery, onion, green pepper and garlic in oil over medium heat until tender, about 5 minutes.

■ Add all other ingredients except spinach and pepper. Bring to boil, reduce heat, cover and simmer for 35 minutes. Remove bay leaves and add spinach.

■ Add pepper to taste. Simmer 10 minutes.

Serves 6.

Lentil Garbanzo Soup

That wonderful aroma of cinnamon, lemon and orange wafting through the house will bring even the most tardy running to the table.

1 cup	cooked garbanzo beans (chick peas)	250 mL
3/4 cup	dried green/brown lentils, rinsed	175 mL
2	leeks (white part plus 1/3 of the green), chopped	2
2	medium carrots, chopped	2
3	celery stalks, chopped	3
6 cups	vegetable stock*	1.5 L
1 tsp	cinnamon	5 mL
	grated rind of one lemon	
	grated rind of one orange	
	juice of one orange	
5 drops	Tabasco (hot red pepper sauce)	5 drops
	salt and pepper to taste	

* Can use bouillon cubes or instant granules. Follow package directions. Recipe for vegetable stock on page 56.

- In a soup pot, place beans, lentils, vegetables and vegetable stock. Bring to boil and reduce heat. Cover and simmer for 40 minutes.

- Add cinnamon, grated lemon and orange rind, and orange juice. Simmer 10 minutes more.

- To serve, garnish with thinly cut orange slices, if desired.

Serves 6.

Roasted Pepper Lentil Soup

We classify this soup in the exotic category. A bit more work because roasting the peppers is a separate step but after one taste, we are certain you'll do it again. Roast extra peppers and use them in Spicy Black Bean Dip (page 23) and Roasted Red Pepper Salad (page 65). Roasted red peppers in jars are now available in grocery stores.

1	each roasted green, red and yellow pepper (see directions below)	1 each
1/2 cup	dried green/brown lentils	125 mL
1 1/2 tsp	chili powder	8 mL
1	can (7 1/2 oz/213 mL) tomato sauce	1
3 cups	water	750 mL
1/4 tsp	salt	1 mL

To roast peppers:

■ Core and seed peppers. Cut in quarters. Place pepper pieces, skin side up on a baking sheet or broiling pan. Broil one side until skin blisters and blackens (do not cremate!) about 5 to 8 minutes.

■ Or, if preferred, you can bake in oven at 500⁰F (260⁰C) for 15 to 20 minutes. Place in paper or plastic bag. Seal and let stand for at least 15 minutes. Peel off the blackened skin.

■ Rinse lentils. In a large saucepan, place lentils and 3 cups water. Simmer, covered for 25 minutes.

■ Cut peppers in strips 1/2 inch (1 cm) long.

■ Add tomato sauce, chili powder, salt and roasted pepper strips. Simmer another 10 minutes.

Serves 4.

Bavarian Lentil Soup

"Do you share recipes?", we inquired one lunch break at a Bavarian restaurant. The unequivocal reply was, "Absolutely not!" A challenge like that sent us to the test kitchen and we feel our version is just as good, if not better, and far friendlier.

6	slices bacon, cut in narrow strips	6
1	medium onion, finely chopped	1
1 cup	dried green/brown lentils, rinsed	250 mL
1	can (28 oz/796 mL) crushed tomatoes	1
6 cups	water	1.5 L
1 Tbsp	paprika	15 mL
1/2 tsp	salt	3 mL
	pepper to taste	
2 Tbsp	light sour cream	25 mL
2 Tbsp	chopped parsley	25 mL

- In skillet, cook bacon until crisp. Remove from pan.
- In the same skillet, sauté onion until tender, about 5 minutes.
- In a large saucepan, combine lentils, tomatoes, water, onions and bacon. Bring to boil, reduce heat, cover and simmer for 45 minutes.
- Add paprika, salt and pepper, and simmer 10 minutes more.
- Serve in individual bowls. Top with sour cream and sprinkle with chopped parsley.

Serves 6.

Asparagus Lentil Soup

The silkiness of the asparagus contrasted with the texture of the lentils gives this soup a special appeal.

5 cups	vegetable stock*	1.25 mL
1 cup	dried green/brown lentils, rinsed	250 mL
1	medium onion, chopped	1
1	celery stalk, diced	1
1/2 tsp	salt	3 mL
8-10	asparagus spears, frozen or fresh	8-10
1/2 cup	grated parmesan or romano cheese	125 mL

* Can use boullion cubes or instant granules, Follow package directions. Recipe for vegetable stock on page 56.

■ In large saucepan, place all ingredients except asparagus and cheese. Simmer, covered, 30 minutes or until lentils are tender. Stir occasionally.

■ Slice each asparagus stalk diagonally into 3 or 4 pieces. Add to soup. If using fresh asparagus, cook 10 minutes. If frozen, cook 4 minutes.

■ Add cheese. Simmer gently until cheese melts, stirring often.

Serves 4.

Lima Bean Soup

Please don't flip by this soup because you think lima beans are large, white, mealy and tough. Find the wonderful, bright green, tender, frozen ones at your market and you'll be searching out more lima recipes.

2 Tbsp	vegetable oil	25 mL
1	large onion, chopped	1
1	large carrot, peeled - cut lengthwise and then into thin slices	1
1	celery stalk, thinly sliced	1
1	green pepper, chopped	1
5 cups	V-8 or tomato juice	1.25 L
1 cup	cooked lima beans*	250 mL
1/4 cup	lemon juice	50 mL
1 tsp	dried thyme	5 mL
1 tsp	salt	5 mL
1/2 tsp	pepper	3 mL

* Use frozen limas or if dried, soak and cook 1/2 cup(125 mL) according to directions on pages 10 and 11.

- In large soup pot, sauté vegetables in oil over medium heat 5 minutes.
- Add V-8 or tomato juice and beans. Simmer, covered, for 30 minutes.
- Add remaining ingredients. Simmer 10 minutes. Taste. Adjust seasonings.

Serves 6.

Carrot Soup

When we served this recipe at a 'test luncheon', some people thought the consistency was just right – others found it too thick. You will have to make a judgment call on the amount of liquid you add.

1 Tbsp	olive oil	15 mL
1	medium onion, chopped	1
12	medium carrots, chopped approx. 2lbs (1 kg)	12
5 cups	vegetable stock*	1.25 L
1 cup	canned chick peas (garbanzo beans), drained and rinsed	250 mL
1/4 cup	tahini (sesame seed paste)	50 mL
1/2 tsp	ground cumin	3 mL
1/2 tsp	salt	3 mL
1/2 cup	orange juice	125 mL
2 tsp	grated orange rind	10 mL
	lots of freshly ground pepper	

* Can use bouillon cubes or instant granules. Follow package instructions. Recipe for vegetable stock on page 56.

- In a large saucepan, sauté onion in oil over medium heat for 5 minutes. Add carrots and sauté for 3 minutes.
- Add remaining ingredients except orange juice and rind. Cover and simmer 20 minutes or until carrots are soft.
- Add orange juice and rind.
- Purée in a food processor or blender.
- Return to saucepan and reheat. Add pepper to taste.

Serves 6.

Romano Italian Sausage Soup

*Suitable only for loggers, oil riggers and... no, no, just kidding!
But it is very hearty so treat it as a main dish for hungry folk.*

1/2 lb	spicy Italian sausage	225 g
1 Tbsp	vegetable oil	15 mL
2	medium onions, chopped	2
1	can (19 oz/540 mL) diced tomatoes	1
2 cups	chicken stock*	500 mL
1/2 cup	red wine	125 mL
1	can (19 oz/540 mL) romano beans, drained and rinsed	1
1 Tbsp	Italian seasoning**	15 mL

* Chicken bouillon cubes or granules can be used. Follow package directions.
** Italian seasoning is a combination of 6 herbs. See Bean Companions on page 13.

- Cut sausage into 1/2"(1 cm) slices.
- In saucepan, brown sausage slices in oil, over medium heat. Remove from pan.
- Sauté onions 3 minutes. Drain excess fat.
- Return sausage slices to pot. Add remaining ingredients. Simmer 10 minutes.

Serves 4.

Romano Brown Rice Soup

Large bowls of this soup would be ample for dinner, accompanied by a leafy side salad and sourdough bread. Also excellent to take to work for lunch.

2 Tbsp	vegetable oil	25 mL
1	medium onion, chopped	1
3	cloves garlic, minced	3
2	carrots, sliced	2
2	celery stalks, sliced	2
1	can (19 oz/540 mL) romano beans, drained and rinsed	1
3	bay leaves	3
1/3 cup	uncooked brown rice	75 mL
1	can (48 oz/1.5 L) tomato juice	1
2 cups	vegetable stock*	500 mL
1 Tbsp	dried oregano	15 mL
1 tsp	dried thyme	5 mL
1 tsp	dried rosemary	5 mL
	salt and pepper to taste	

* Can use bouillon cubes or instant granules. Follow package instructions. Recipe for vegetable stock on page 56.

- In large soup pot, sauté onion and garlic in oil over medium heat for 3 minutes.
- Add vegetables, beans, bay leaves, rice and liquid. Simmer, covered, for 40 minutes.
- Add herbs. Simmer, covered, 10 minutes more.
- Remove bay leaves. Taste. Add salt and pepper if necessary.

Serves 6.

Spanish Vegetable Soup

This soup was put in the outstanding category by our testers. Its taste lives up to its appearance. Could be a great beginning to a special dinner or the main attraction of a summer lunch.

1 Tbsp	olive oil	15 ml
1	medium onion, chopped	1
2	medium carrots, chopped	2
1	stalk celery, chopped	1
1	red pepper, chopped	1
4 cups	vegetable stock*	1 L
1 cup	cauliflower flowerets**	250 mL
1 cup	broccoli flowerets**	250 mL
2 Tbsp	chopped black olives	25 mL
2 Tbsp	tomato paste	25 mL
1 Tbsp	red wine vinegar	15 mL
1 tsp	capers	5 mL
1 cup	cooked chick peas (garbanzo beans)	250 mL
1/2 tsp	each: dried basil, oregano and thyme	3 mL

* Can use boullion cubes or instant granules. Follow package directions. Recipe for vegetable stock, page 56.
** Make flowerets small, bite-sized pieces.

■ In large saucepan, sauté onion, carrots, celery and red pepper in oil over medium heat for 5 minutes.

■ Add other ingredients except capers, beans and herbs. Bring to boil and reduce heat. Cover and simmer about 10 minutes until cauliflower and broccoli are nearly cooked.

■ Add other ingredients and heat about 5 minutes or until beans are warmed through.

Serves 4-6.

Kidney Bean Asiago Soup

A truly gourmet soup, but so easy to prepare. We feel you must experience the combination of beans and asiago cheese. This sophisticated Italian cheese is now more widely available. The recipe is easily doubled.

1	small onion, chopped	1
1	can (l4 oz/398 mL) tomato sauce	1
1	can (14 oz/398 mL) kidney beans, drained and rinsed	1
1	can (14oz/398 mL) water	1
1 tsp	Italian seasoning*	5 mL
1 oz	Asiago cheese	30 g

* A combination of herbs, found on the spice shelves of your grocery stores. See Bean Companions, page 13.

- Combine onion, tomato sauce, water and Italian seasoning in a saucepan. Simmer for 20 minutes.
- Add kidney beans and simmer for 5 minutes more.
- In a food processor or blender, purée all the soup mixture. Return to saucepan.
- Coarsely grate cheese (save a little for garnish). Add the rest to the soup mixture. Simmer gently until the cheese melts, stirring often.
- Serve in small bowls. Sprinkle with the extra cheese.

3 small servings.

Pinto Bean Soup

What can be better on a cold winter day than a stick-to-the-ribs soup such as this one? Serve with some peasant bread to complete this simple but nourishing meal.

2 cups	cooked pinto beans*	500 mL
1 Tbsp	vegetable oil	15 mL
1	medium onion, chopped	1
1	medium zucchini, chopped	1
1	large potato, chopped	1
4 cups	vegetable stock**	1 L
1 cup	canned crushed tomatoes	250 mL
2 tsp	fine herbs	10 mL
1 tsp	salt	5 mL

* If using dried beans, soak and cook 3/4 (175 mL) cup according to directions on pages 10 and 11.
** Can use vegetable bouillon cubes or instant granules. Follow package instructions. Recipe for vegetable stock on page 56.

■ In soup pot, sauté onion in oil over medium heat for 5 minutes.

■ Add all other ingredients, except tomatoes, fine herbs and salt. Bring to boil, reduce heat. Cover and simmer 20 minutes or until potatoes are cooked.

■ Add tomatoes, fine herbs and salt. Simmer 5 minutes more.

Serves 4.

Fiesta Taco Soup

This meal-in-a-bowl soup is quickly assembled but best made a day ahead, to let the flavors meld. Make it and let it simmer while you're preparing tonight's dinner. Tortilla strips (page 17) are a natural partner.

1/2 lb	lean ground beef	225 g
6 cups	water	1.5 L
1	medium onion, chopped	1
2	medium potatoes, diced	2
3	carrots, diced	3
1	can (14 oz/398 mL) diced tomatoes	1
1 cup	cooked pinto beans*	250 mL
1	package (1 3/8 oz/40 g) taco seasoning mix	1
1 tsp	chili powder	5 mL
	salt and pepper to taste	

* Can use 1/3 cup (75 mL) of dried beans, soaked and cooked according to directions on pages 10 and 11.

- In a large saucepan, brown meat.
- Add remaining ingredients. Simmer, covered, until potatoes and carrots are soft, about 40 minutes.

Serves 6.

Turkey Soup

A mild flavored soup, so spice it up if you're so inclined. It does need turkey stock to do it justice. We suggest that you make the stock after one of your festive dinners and freeze it for future use.

1/2 cup	dried navy beans*	125 mL
2 Tbsp	vegetable oil	25 mL
1	medium onion, chopped	1
4	carrots, chopped	4
2 cups	chopped mushrooms	500 mL
2	cloves garlic, minced	2
7 cups	turkey stock (recipe below)	1.75 L
1 cup	turkey bits (can use more)	250 mL
1 tsp	dried marjoram	5 mL
1 tsp	paprika	5 mL
1 tsp	salt	5 mL
	lots of freshly ground pepper	

* Quick soak beans according to directions on page 10. Can use 1 cup (250 mL) of canned navy beans.

- In soup pot, sauté onion, carrots, mushrooms and garlic, in oil over medium heat for 5 minutes.
- Add turkey stock and beans and simmer for 40 minutes.
- Add remaining ingredients and simmer 10 minutes more.

Serves 6.

Turkey stock:

- In large pot, add 12 cups of water to the turkey bones. Chop and add one onion, 2 celery stalks with leaves and 2 carrots. Add 2 bay leaves.
- Simmer 1 hour. Strain. Refrigerate until fat congeals. Remove fat. Freeze if not going to use immediately.

Italian White Bean Soup

This is a super supper soup. Gorgonzola cheese is what makes it so special. It is expensive but a little goes a long way. We have substituted blue cheese when gorgonzola wasn't available.

1 Tbsp	olive oil	15 mL
1	small onion, chopped	1
2	stalks celery, chopped	2
2	medium carrots, chopped	2
2	medium leeks (white part plus 1/3 of the green), chopped	2
1 1/3 cups	cooked navy beans*	325 mL
4 cups	vegetable stock**	1 L
1/3 cup	skim milk	75 mL
1/3 cup	Gorgonzola cheese, crumbled	75 mL
1/2 tsp	thyme	3 mL
	lots of freshly ground pepper	
1/4 cup	parsley, chopped	50 mL

* If using dried beans, quick soak and cook 1/2 cup (125 mL) according to directions on pages 10 and 11.
** Can use bouillon cubes or granules. Follow package directions. Recipe for vegetable stock on page 56.

- In a large saucepan, sauté vegetables in oil over medium heat for 5 minutes.
- Add beans and vegetable stock. Simmer 30 minutes.
- Add milk, cheese, thyme, pepper and half the parsley. Simmer, stirring often until cheese melts, about 5 minutes.
- Serve garnished with reserved parsley.

Serves 4.

White Bean Borscht

Russia and the West embrace for a 'beany' variation of this traditional soup. Canned beets instead of fresh make preparation speedier and less messy. Fresh dill is wonderful, if available.

2 Tbsp	vegetable oil	25 mL
1	large onion, sliced in thin rounds	1
2	cloves garlic, minced	2
1 cup	shredded green cabbage	250 mL
4 cups	vegetable stock*	1 L
2	medium cooked beets, grated	2
3/4 cup	cooked navy beans	175 mL
1/4 cup	red wine vinegar	50 mL
1 Tbsp	fresh dill**	15 mL
	salt and pepper to taste	
	low fat sour cream	

* Can use bouillon cubes or instant granules Follow package instructions. Recipe for vegetable stock on page 56.
** Use 1 tsp (5 mL) dried dill if fresh is unavailable.

- ■ In soup pot, sauté onion and garlic in oil over medium heat for 3 minutes.

- ■ Add cabbage, vegetable stock, beets and beans. Simmer, covered, for 30 minutes.

- ■ Add remaining ingredients. Simmer 5 minutes more. Taste and adjust seasonings.

- ■ Serve in bowls. Garnish with a dollop of sour cream and extra dill if desired.

Serves 4.

- 51 -

Broccoli Bean Soup

Here is a creamy broccoli soup without the calories. White beans are the thickener. Delicious served cold, too.

4 cups	chopped broccoli	1 L
1	medium onion, chopped	1
1 Tbsp	olive oil	15 mL
3 1/2 cups	vegetable stock*	875 mL
1 cup	cooked navy beans**	250 mL
1	bay leaf	1
1/2 tsp	allspice	3 mL
1/2 tsp	thyme	3 mL
1/4 cup	low fat yogurt	50 mL
	broccoli flower buds for garnish	

* Can use bouillion cubes or instant granules. Follow package instructions. Recipe for vegetable stock on page 56.
** If using dried beans, soak and cook 1/2 cup (125 mL) according to directions on pages 10 and 11.

■ To prepare broccoli, cut off tough bottoms ends. Peel the remaining stocks and coarsely chop stems and tops. Reserve 2 flowerets to use as small flower buds for garnish.

■ In a large saucepan, sauté onion in oil over medium heat for 5 minutes.

■ Add remaining ingredients and simmer, covered, for 20 minutes.

■ Cool slightly and purée in food processor or blender until smooth. Return to saucepan and reheat.

■ Serve in bowls with a dollop of yogurt and sprinkle with the reserved broccoli which has been separated into flower buds.

Serves 4.

Lime White Bean Soup

A quiet light green soup that is perfect for lunch. The subtle bite of fresh lime juice sets it apart.

1 Tbsp	vegetable oil	15 mL
1	medium onion, chopped	1
2	cloves garlic, minced	2
6 cups	chicken stock*	1.5 L
1	boneless chicken breast, skinned and diced	1
1	can (4 oz/114 mL) diced green chilies, drained	1
1 cup	cooked navy or Great Northern beans**	250 mL
1/4 cup	lime juice	50 mL
1 tsp	dried marjoram	5 mL
1/2 tsp	dried thyme	3 mL
	chopped parsley	

* Can use chicken bouillon cubes or granules. Follow package instructions.
** If using dried beans, soak and cook 1/2 cup (125 mL) of dried beans according to directions on pages 10 and 11.

■ In soup pot or large saucepan, sauté onion and garlic in oil over medium heat for 3 minutes.

■ Add remaining ingredients except parsley. Simmer, uncovered, for 15 minutes.

■ Serve in colorful bowls. Garnish with chopped parsley.

Serves 4.

Gazpacho with White Beans

A cold vegetable soup – so delicious it's a shame we only think about it in the summer. Ours is slightly chunky but if you like it smooth, just leave the food processor running a few seconds longer. Add more tomato or V-8 juice for a thinner version and more red wine vinegar for extra bite.

3	ripe tomatoes, peeled and chopped	3
1	cucumber, peeled and chopped	1
1	green pepper, chopped	1
1	medium onion, chopped	1
3	cloves garlic, minced	3
1/2 cup	olive oil	125 mL
1/3 cup	red wine vinegar	75 mL
2 cups	tomato or V-8 juice	500 mL
1 tsp	salt	5 mL
1 cup	cooked navy or Great Northern beans*	250 mL

*If using dried beans, soak and cook 1/2 cup (125 mL), following directions on pages 10 and 11.

- ■ Place all ingredients except the beans in a large food processor. Whirl for 6 seconds or until vegetables are tiny chunks.
- ■ Pour into an attractive bowl. Add beans and stir well.
- ■ Refrigerate for at least 2 hours or until well chilled.
- ■ Suggested garnishes:
  - chopped parsley
  - dollop of sour cream
  - sliced green onions

Serves 4-6.

Kale Portuguese Soup

A thick, hearty soup that's a meal in a bowl. You can make it as spicy as you wish by adding a little or a lot of red pepper flakes. This is a winter soup when kale is available everywhere.

1/4 lb	low fat, mild Italian sausage	100 g
2 tsp	olive oil	10 mL
1	large onion, chopped	1
2	cloves garlic, minced	2
3	medium potatoes, peeled and cut in 1/2" (1 cm) chunks	3
1	bay leaf	1
4 cups	chicken stock*	1
	pinch of red pepper flakes**	
4	large kale leaves, stems removed, cut in I " (2 cm) slices	4
1 cup	cooked navy beans***	250 mL
	salt and pepper to taste	

* Can use chicken bouillon cubes or instant granules. Follow package instructions.
** Use sparingly. You can always add more.
*** If using dried beans, soak and cook 1/2 cup (125 mL) as directed on pages 10 and 11.

- In large heavy saucepan, brown sausages. Remove from pan. Allow to cool. Cut in half lengthwise and then into 1/2" (1 cm) slices.

- Add olive oil and sauté onions and garlic over medium heat for 5 minutes.

- Add sausages, potatoes, chicken stock, bay leaf and red pepper flakes. Bring to boil and simmer, covered, for 20 minutes.

- Remove bay leaf. Add kale, beans, salt and pepper. Simmer 5 minutes more.

Serves 4.

Vegetable Stock

When a soup calls for vegetable stock, you can make your own or use bouillon cubes or instant granules to which you add water. Here is a very basic recipe for a homemade stock.

1	large onion, chopped.	1
2	large carrots, chopped	2
3	celery stalks, chopped, with leaves	3
8 cups	water	2 L
2	bay leaves	2
1/4 cup	chopped parsley, optional	50 mL
1 tsp	dried thyme	5 mL
1/2 tsp	salt	2 mL

- In large soup pot, combine all ingredients. Bring to boil, cover and simmer for 1 hour.
- Strain. Discard vegetables.
- Freezes well.

Makes 7-8 cups.

Salads

Salads

Mexi-Cali Bean Salad

A presentation plus is serving this salad in tortilla shells. They are easy to make yourself (recipe below) or else buy them prebaked.

3 cups	cooked black beans*	375 mL
1 cup	artichoke hearts, coarsely chopped	250 mL
1	large red pepper, chopped	1
1/2 cup	chopped cilantro	125 mL
4	green onions, chopped	4
	shredded lettuce	
Dressing:		
1/4 cup	olive oil	50 mL
3 Tbsp	lime juice	45 mL
2 tsp	liquid honey	10 mL
	pinch of red pepper flakes	

* If using dried beans, soak and cook 1 1/4 cups (300 mL) according to directions on pages 10 and 11.

■ In medium bowl, combine all ingredients except dressing.
■ In tightly lidded jar, combine dressing ingredients. Shake well and pour over salad mixture and toss lightly.

To serve:

■ Line a salad bowl with lettuce leaves and spoon salad mixture in. Or place shredded lettuce in individual tortilla bowls (see below). Spoon in salad mixture. Garnish with sour cream, if desired.

Serves 4-6

To make tortilla salad bowls:

   Use 8" (20 cm) or 10' (25 cm) flour tortillas, plain or whole wheat
■ Turn a 2 cup (500 mL) glass measuring cup upside down. Oil lightly. Centre the tortilla over it. Microwave, uncovered, on high for 30-45 seconds or until tortilla is soft.
■ Using oven mitts, gently press the tortilla around the sides of the measuring cup. Microwave on high 1minute more or until brown patches appear.
■ Remove the tortilla shell from the cup. Cool. Make extra because they keep well.

Pinto Bean Salad

This is a substantial salad with great color appeal. Suitable for lunch or for a vegetarian dinner with rice. Consider doubling this recipe as it keeps well for three days.

2 cups	cooked pinto beans*	500 mL
1/2 cup	thinly sliced red onion	125 mL
1	can (4.5 oz/127 mL) chopped green chilies, drained	1
2	carrots, peeled and coarsely grated	2
1	stalk celery, sliced	1
1/3 cup	chopped parsley	75 mL
	freshly ground pepper	
Dressing:		
3 Tbsp	olive oil	45 mL
2 Tbsp	red wine vinegar	25 mL
1 tsp	dried oregano**	5 mL
1	clove garlic, minced	1

*If using dried beans, soak and cook 3/4 cup (175 mL) according to directions on pages 10 and 11.
** If fresh oregano is available, use 1 Tbsp chopped.

- If using canned beans, drain and rinse.
- In a pottery bowl, combine beans, vegetables, parsley and pepper.
- In tightly lidded jar, combine dressing ingredients. Shake well.
- Pour over beans and vegetables. Toss lightly.
- Let stand for one hour in the refrigerator. Can be made the day before serving.

Serves 6.

Mexican Stir-Fry Salad

Taking only 10 minutes to slice and 10 minutes to cook, this is a perfect summer supper salad. Any extra can be your next day's lunch. Spoon into a pita pocket, eat cold or microwave one minute (lettuce omitted).

1 Tbsp	vegetable oil	15 mL
1	clove garlic, minced	1
1 tsp	each: cumin, oregano, chili	5 mL
1	medium onion, sliced vertically	1
1	red pepper, sliced lengthwise	1
1/2 lb	flank or sirloin steak, cut in	225 g
	1/4"(.5 cm) strips*	
1 Tbsp	canned diced green chilies	15 mL
1 cup	cooked black beans**	250 mL
3 cups	romaine lettuce,	750 mL
	cut in 1"(2.5 cm) strips	

* Steak is more easily cut if slightly frozen.
** If using dried beans, soak and cook 1/2 cup (125 mL) according to directions on pages 10 and 11.

- Combine oil, garlic and spices in small bowl.
- Pour oil and spice mixture into skillet. Sauté onion and red pepper over medium heat for 5 minutes. Remove from pan.
- Heat an additional 1 Tbsp (15 mL) of oil in skillet and stir-fry steak to desired doneness.
- Add reserved vegetables, chilies, and beans. Heat through.
- Serve over lettuce.

Serves 4.

Black Bean Orzo Salad

Orzo is a tiny rice-like pasta which you can usually find in packages on the pasta shelves or in bulk. Experiment with it in soups, main dishes and refreshing salads, such as this one.

3/4 cup	orzo	175 mL
1 cup	cooked black beans*	250 mL
1/2 cup	sundried tomatoes, chopped	125 mL
3	green onions, sliced	3
1/2 cup	chopped cilantro	125 mL
Dressing:		
1/4 cup	lime juice, fresh if possible	50 mL
3 Tbsp	vegetable oil	45 mL
1	clove garlic, minced	1
1/4 tsp	salt	1 mL

* If using dried beans soak and cook 1/2 cup (125 mL) according to directions on pages 10 and 11.

- In a large saucepan, bring 4 cups of water to a rolling boil (approximately five times the amount of water to pasta.) Cook orzo for 10 minutes. Drain and rinse.
- Place orzo in medium bowl and add remaining ingredients except dressing. Mix.
- In tightly lidded jar, combine dressing ingredients. Shake well.
- Add to orzo bean mixture. Toss lightly. Refrigerate 1 hour.
- Serve in a bowl lined with salad greens.

Serves 4.

Black Bean Pasta Salad

Served at a 'bean tasters' luncheon, this salad was given rave reviews. It is most attractive when bow pasta is used and it is presented on a colorful platter.

1 cup	dried bow pasta*	250 mL
1 cup	cooked black beans	250 mL
1/2 cup	marinated artichoke hearts, drained and chopped	125 mL
2	Roma tomatoes, chopped	2
1/2 cup	sundried tomatoes, chopped	125 mL
1 cup	parmesan cheese, coarsely grated	250 mL
1/3 cup	chopped fresh basil	75 mL
	freshly ground pepper	
Dressing:		
1/4 cup	olive oil	50 mL
1 Tbsp	lemon juice	I5 mL

* If bow pasta is unavailable, use rotini or other small pasta.

- Cook pasta in boiling water until done, 8 to 10 minutes. Drain.
- In medium bowl, combine other salad ingredients, except basil.
- In tightly lidded jar, combine oil and lemon juice. Shake well.
- Add dressing to salad ingredients. Cover and refrigerate.
- Take salad out of refrigerator an hour before serving.
- Just before serving, add basil and toss lightly. Serve on a platter and garnish edges with extra basil.

Serves 6.

Mimi's Three Bean Salad

Often offered but seldom taken are the family recipes suggested to us on our travels. Here is the exception. This salad is a staple of an exceptional lady from Nashville. Nothing is changed, nothing needs improving.

1	can (19 oz/540 mL) kidney beans	1
1	can (19 oz/540 mL) chick peas (garbanzo beans)	1
1	can (19 oz/540 mL) black beans	1
2	celery stalks, sliced in thin rounds	2
1	red onion, diced	1
1	tomato, seeds removed and diced	1
1 cup	frozen corn, cooked	250 mL
3/4 cup	thick and chunky salsa	175 mL
Dressing:		
1/2 cup	vegetable oil	125 mL
1/4 cup	lime juice (fresh if possible)	50 mL
1 1/2 tsp	chili powder	8 mL
1/2 tsp	salt	3 mL
1/2 tsp	ground cumin	3 mL

■ Drain and rinse canned beans.

■ Place all ingredients except dressing in a large bowl. Stir well.

■ In a tightly lidded jar, combine dressing ingredients. Shake well. Add to bean mixture.

■ Chill in refrigerator for at least one hour before serving.

■ Serve in a lettuce-lined salad bowl.

Serves 6-8.

Lima Bean Salad

The words 'elegant' and 'beans' hardly ever appear in the same sentence. However, the blending of the soft green of the limas with the darker green of the parsley, set off by black olives, makes this salad look very upscale. Try presenting it in a white, low rimmed serving bowl.

2 cups	frozen lima beans	500 mL
1/2 cup	diced red onion	125 mL
1 cup	black olives, cut in quarters	250 mL
1 cup	chopped parsley	250 mL
Dressing:		
2 Tbsp	vegetable oil	25 mL
1 Tbsp	white wine vinegar	15 mL
2 Tbsp	orange juice	25 mL
2	cloves garlic, minced	2
	salt and pepper to taste	

- Cook lima beans according to package directions. Drain and cool.
- Add onion, olives and parsley. Mix well.
- In tightly lidded jar, combine dressing ingredients. Shake well. Add to salad ingredients.
- Cover and refrigerate until chilled.

Serves 4-6.

Roasted Pepper Salad

Having experimented with different methods of roasting peppers, we find this one fills the criteria of an Easy Beans cookbook – simple and fast. Serve this attractive salad for lunch.

3	roasted peppers, 1 green ,	3
	1 red, 1 yellow (recipe below)	
1 Tbsp	chopped fresh basil	15 mL
1 cup	canned chick peas,	250 mL
	drained and rinsed	
1	head romaine lettuce	1
Dressing:		
2 Tbsp	olive oil	25 mL
2 Tbsp	red wine vinegar	25 mL
2	cloves garlic, minced	2
	freshly ground pepper	

To roast peppers:
- Core and seed peppers. Cut peppers in quarters.
- Place on baking sheet, skin side up. Broil for 5 to 7 minutes until skin blisters and blackens (don't cremate!). If preferred, you can bake in oven at 500°F (260°C) for 15 to 20 minutes.
- Place in paper or plastic bag and seal for 10 to 15 minutes. Remove and peel off blackened skin.

- Cut peppers in thin strips lengthwise and then in half.
- In tightly lidded jar, combine dressing ingredients.
- In medium bowl, combine roasted pepper strips, basil and chick peas. Cover with dressing. Marinate overnight in refrigerator.
- Wash and cut lettuce in l"(2.5 cm) strips.
- Place lettuce in salad bowl or on individual plates. Spoon pepper mixture over it.

Serves 6.

Turkish Chick Pea Salad

This salad is a winning accompaniment to other dishes. It would be a natural served with grilled fish. Experiment with the other herbs to achieve different flavors.

1	can (19 oz/540 mL) chick peas (garbanzo beans), drained and rinsed	1
1 cup	finely diced red onions	250 mL
Dressing:		
1/4 cup	olive oil	50 mL
3 Tbsp	red wine vinegar	45 mL
1 Tbsp	lemon juice	15 mL
1 Tbsp	fresh thyme, finely chopped*	15 mL
2 Tbsp	fresh tarragon, finely chopped*	30 mL
1 Tbsp	parsley, finely chopped*	15 mL

* Try any combination of fresh herbs, but don't use less than 1/4 cup (50 mL).

- In a bowl, combine chick peas and onions.
- In tightly lidded jar, combine all dressing ingredients. Shake well.
- Add dressing to chick peas and stir gently. Let stand for 1 hour.
- Serve in a lettuce-lined bowl.

Serves 6.

Curried Potato Salad

Some combinations say yes the first time you test them. This is definitely one. Please throw out any ancient curry powder and treat yourself to a good Indian variety; the taste difference is astonishing. Easily doubled or tripled, it is perfect for picnics.

15	snow peas	15
4	large cooked potatoes, unpeeled	4
1	red onion, diced	1
1 cup	canned chick peas, drained and rinsed	250 mL
Dressing:		
3 Tbsp	olive oil	45 mL
2 Tbsp	lemon juice	25 mL
2 tsp	grated fresh ginger*	10 mL
1 tsp	curry powder	5 mL
1/2 tsp	dry mustard	3 mL
1/2 tsp	salt	3 mL

* If fresh ginger is not available, use 1/2 tsp (3 mL) ginger powder.

- Wash and cut tips off snow peas. Steam cook for 1 minute. Cool and slice each one into 4 diagonal pieces.
- Peel cooked potatoes. Cut into small chunks.
- In medium bowl combine all ingredients except dressing.
- In tightly lidded jar, combine dressing ingredients. Shake well. Add to vegetables and beans. Stir gently.
- Store in refrigerator. To serve, place in a lettuce lined glass bowl. Garnish with red onion slices.

Serves 4-6.

Pesto White Bean Salad

Nothing beats homemade pesto. This salad only uses 1/4 cup (50 mL) so squirrel away the extra for other recipes by storing in a covered container in the refrigerator. If time is a factor, buy any of the pestos available in the stores.

1 cup	colored rotini	250 mL
1 cup	cooked chick peas (garbanzo beans)*	250 mL
1 cup	cooked white beans (Great Northern or navy)*	250 mL
1	red pepper, chopped	1
1/4 cup	pesto sauce (recipe follows)	50 mL
1 tsp	lemon juice	5 mL
Pesto Sauce:		
2 cups	fresh basil, tightly packed	500 mL
1/4 cup	grated romano cheese	50 mL
1/4 cup	pine nuts	50 mL
3	cloves garlic, minced	3
3 Tbsp	olive oil	45 mL
1 Tbsp	lemon juice	15 mL

* If using dried beans, soak and cook 1/2 cup (125 mL) according to directions on pages 10 and 11.

■ Cook rotini in boiling water until tender. Drain and cool.

■ In salad bowl, combine rotini, beans and red peppers.

■ In food processor or blender, combine all pesto sauce ingredients. Blend until smooth.

■ Combine pesto sauce and lemon juice. Toss gently with bean mixture.

■ Let stand for several hours for the best flavor.

Serves 4-6.

Wild Rice & Bean Salad

How could this salad miss with ingredients like wild rice, snow peas and sundried tomatoes? Purchase these tomatoes either preserved in oil or dried but don't forget the dried ones must be soaked for a few minutes before using.

1	pkg (6 oz/170 g) wild rice mix	1
1 1/2 cups	cooked navy beans*	375 mL
18	snow peas, cut in 1/2 "(1 cm) pieces	18
1	small green pepper, chopped	1
2	green onions, chopped	2
9	sundried tomatoes, chopped finely	9
Dressing:		
3 Tbsp	olive oil	45 mL
3 Tbsp	balsamic vinegar	45 mL
1 1/2 tsp	sugar	8 mL
1/2 tsp	dry mustard	3 mL

* If using dried beans, soak and cook 3/4 cup (175 mL) as directed on pages 10 and 11.

■ Wash and cut tips off snow peas. Steam cook for 2 minutes. Rinse in cold water.

■ Cook wild rice mix according to package instructions. Cool.

■ Combine all salad ingredients.

■ In tightly lidded jar, combine dressing ingredients. Shake well. Pour over salad mixture and toss lightly.

Serves 4-6.

White Bean Crab Salad

Fresh crab would be wonderful but the imitation crab – available in the fish section – is also very acceptable. Serve in a low sided, brightly colored dish for maximum presentation.

1	can (4 oz/113 g) crab, drained	1
2 cups	cooked navy beans*	500 mL
1/2 cup	black olives, sliced	125 mL
1	small green pepper, thinly sliced	1
1/2 cup	chopped parsley	125 mL
Dressing:		
1/2 cup	lemon juice	125 mL
1/3 cup	vegetable oil	75 mL
1 Tbsp	Dijon mustard	15 mL
1/2 tsp	salt	3 mL

* If using dried beans, soak and cook 3/4 cup (175 mL) according to directions on pages 10 and 11.

■ In a bowl, combine salad ingredients.

■ In tightly lidded jar, combine dressing ingredients. Shake well and add to salad ingredients. Mix well. Chill in refrigerator.

Serves 4.

Spinach White Bean Salad

*"You two really do like feta cheese, don't you?", was an often heard remark from cooks perusing our first book, **Easy Beans**. We confess it's true but this time around we've been more reticent. We experimented with other cheeses when testing this salad but our testers gave thumbs-up to our good old favorite.*

1/2	pkg fresh (10 oz/283 g) or 1 bunch spinach	1/2
1	small red onion, sliced thinly	1
3/4 cup	walnuts, chopped coarsely	175 mL
3/4 cup	cooked navy beans*	175 mL
1/2 cup	crumbled feta cheese	125 mL
Dressing:		
1/4 cup	red wine vinegar	50 mL
1/4 cup	vegetable oil	50 mL
2	cloves garlic, minced	2
1/2 tsp	sugar	3 mL
	salt and pepper to taste	

* If using dried beans, soak and cook 1/3 of a cup (75 mL) according to directions on pages 10 and 11.

■ If using unpackaged spinach, rinse and drain well. Pat dry with a paper towel.

■ Tear spinach into bite sized pieces and place in glass salad bowl. Add remaining ingredients except dressing.

■ In a tightly lidded jar, combine dressing ingredients. Shake well.

■ Just before serving, pour dressing over salad and toss gently to prevent nuts and beans from slipping to the bottom of bowl.

Serves 4.

Asian Vegetable Salad

Compliments fly when this very attractive and healthy salad appears at the table. A nice change from the routine tossed salad. It can also be served on six individual side plates.

1 cup	broccoli flowerets	250 mL
10	mushrooms, thinly sliced	10
1	red pepper, cut in long thin strips	1
1	yellow pepper, cut in long thin strips	1
2	green onions, chopped	2
1/2 cup	cooked navy beans*	125 mL
1	head romaine lettuce	1
2 Tbsp	sesame seeds, toasted**	25 mL
Dressing:		
2 Tbsp	vegetable oil	25 mL
2 Tbsp	rice vinegar	25 mL
1 Tbsp	soy sauce	15 mL
1 tsp	honey	5 mL
1	clove garlic, minced	1

* Any leftover beans can be used.
** To toast sesame seeds, place on baking sheet and bake for 10 to 15 minutes at 275⁰F (140⁰C). Watch them so they don't get too brown.

■ Steam broccoli flowerets for 3 minutes. They should still be green and crunchy.

■ In tightly lidded jar, combine dressing ingredients.

■ In medium sized bowl, combine beans and vegetables except lettuce. Add dressing. Toss to coat.

■ Tear lettuce into bite-size pieces. Place in salad bowl. Top with vegetable mixture and sprinkle with sesame seeds.

Serves 6.

Balsamic Beans on Tomatoes

No question about it – balsamic vinegar is a bean's best friend. The longer they spend together, the tastier the beans become. If you make extra marinade you can use it as a dip for focaccia bread.

1 cup	cooked black beans*	250 mL
1 cup	cooked navy beans*	250 mL
1 cup	cooked red kidney beans**	250 mL
4	green onions, sliced	4
1/4 cup	chopped fresh basil	50 mL
4	large ripe tomatoes	4
Marinade:		
1 Tbsp	olive oil	15 mL
2 Tbsp	orange juice	25 mL
3 Tbsp	balsamic vinegar	45 mL

* If using dried beans, soak and cook 1/2 cup (125 mL) each according to directions on pages 10 and 11.
** Can substitute small red Mexican beans.

- In medium bowl, mix beans, onions and basil together.
- In separate small bowl, mix marinade. Add to beans and refrigerate for at least three hours (overnight is even better). Stir occasionally.
- When ready to serve, cut tomatoes in 1/2" (1 cm) slices.
- Arrange on large flat dish. Heap marinated bean mixture on top of each slice.

Serves 6.

Bread Salad With Beans

The traditional Italian Panzanella Salad always looked like it had been out in the rain too long. North Americans don't like 'mushy' but we definitely love cubes of toasted bread, so here is the result of our much enjoyed testing.

1/2	loaf, day old French or Italian bread	1/2
2	large, ripe tomatoes	2
1 cup	unpeeled cucumber	250 mL
1/2 cup	chopped parsley	125 mL
4	green onions, chopped	4
1/2	green pepper, chopped	1/2
1 cup	cooked navy beans*	125 mL
1/2 cup	chopped fresh basil	125 mL
Dressing:		
1/4 cup	vegetable oil	50 mL
1/3 cup	red wine vinegar	75 mL
2	cloves garlic, minced	2
1/2 tsp	sugar	3 mL
	salt and pepper to taste	

* If using dried beans, soak and cook 1/2 cup (125 mL) according to directions on pages 10 and 11.

- Cut bread into 1/2"x 1/2" (1 cm x 1 cm) cubes. Place cubes on baking sheet and bake at 325⁰F (160⁰C) for 10 -15 minutes, or until brown. Stir once.
- Remove seeds and pulp from both the tomatoes and cucumber. Invert tomatoes on a plate to drain. Once drained, dice cucumbers and tomatoes.
- In medium salad bowl, mix all ingredients together except dressing and bread. In tightly lidded jar, combine all dressing ingredients. Shake well.

To serve:

- If you like the bread cubes moist, mix them into the salad. Stir in dressing. Let sit for at least 15 minutes.
- Or, for a drier salad, toss vegetables, beans and dressing together. Add bread cubes and serve immediately.

Serves 4.

Red Cabbage Salad

An excellent buffet salad. The perky red and white coloring is an appealing contrast to the traditional green salad.

6 cups	shredded red cabbage	1.5 L
1/2 cup	crumbled feta cheese	125 mL
5	green onions, chopped	5
1/2 cup	chopped parsley	125 mL
1/2 cup	cooked navy beans	125 mL
Dressing:		
1/4 cup	vegetable oil	50 mL
2 Tbsp	cider vinegar	25 mL
1 tsp	Dijon mustard	5 mL
1/2 tsp	sugar	2 mL

- In a large bowl, combine salad ingredients.
- In a tightly lidded jar, combine dressing ingredients. Shake well.
- Combine dressing with salad ingredients. Toss lightly.

Serves 6.

Eastern Wild Rice Salad

If you have never tried adzuki beans, you are in for a treat. They have a sweet, rather nutty flavor. They may not be as readily available as some of the more common beans but try a popular bulk food store or check the canned section in your supermarket.

1	package (6 oz/180 g) long grain and wild rice mix	1
1 1/2 cups	cooked adzuki beans*	375 mL
6	green onions, chopped	6
1	green pepper, chopped	1
12	slices English cucumber, cut in half	12
1	can (8 oz/227 mL) sliced water chestnuts, drained	1
Dressing:		
1/4 cup	vegetable oil	50 mL
1 Tbsp	cider vinegar	15 mL
1 Tbsp	lemon juice	15 mL
1 Tbsp	teriyaki sauce**	15 mL
1 Tbsp	lime juice	15 mL
1 tsp	honey	5 mL

* If using dried beans, soak and cook 3/4 cup (175 mL) according to directions on pages 10 and 11.
** You can use soy sauce instead of teriyaki, but add 1 tsp (5 mL) of honey.

■ Cook long grain and wild rice mix as directed on the package.

■ In medium bowl, combine rice with beans, vegetables and water chestnuts.

■ In a tightly lidded jar, combine dressing ingredients. Shake well. Pour over bean and rice mixture and toss lightly.

■ Refrigerate for several hours before serving. Keeps for 3 days.

Serves 8.

Oriental Bean Salad

Our testers rated this salad 11 out of 10. The satisfying crunch of the noodles, the freshness of the bean sprouts and the soy sauce dressing all conjured up happy thoughts of past Chinese dishes. It will keep for one extra day but we have never experienced leftovers.

2 cups	shredded green cabbage	500 mL
6	green onions, sliced	6
2 cups	bean sprouts	500 mL
1 cup	chopped broccoli flowerets	250 mL
1 cup	chopped cucumber	250 mL
1 cup	cooked adzuki beans*	250 mL
1 cup	dried instant noodles	250 mL
1/2 cup	toasted sesame seeds**	125 mL
Dressing:		
1/3 cup	vegetable oil	75 mL
1/4 cup	white vinegar	50 mL
3 Tbsp	soy sauce	45 mL
1 Tbsp	sugar	15 mL
1 tsp	salt	5 mL

* If using dried beans, soak and cook 1/2 cup (125 mL) according to directions on pages 10 and 11.
** To toast sesame seeds, put on baking sheet and bake for 10 to 15 minutes at 275⁰F (140⁰C). Watch them so they don't get too brown.

■ In large bowl, combine vegetables and beans.

■ In tightly lidded jar, combine dressing ingredients. Shake well.

■ Combine vegetables and dressing. Toss lightly.

■ Just before serving, add noodles and sesame seeds.

Serves 6-8.

Adzuki Fruit Salad

This is a perfect salad for a group. Dried cranberries and pecans are a little pricey but raisins and walnuts substitute very well. It's important to use the best curry powder available.

4 cups	cooked brown rice	1 L
1	carrot, finely chopped	1
1	apple, unpeeled and chopped	1
1 cup	fresh or canned pineapple, chopped	250 mL
1 cup	cooked adzuki beans*	250 mL
1	red pepper, finely chopped	1
1/2 cup	dried cranberries	125 mL
1/2 cup	pecan pieces	125 mL
Dressing:		
1/4 cup	vegetable oil	50 mL
1/4 cup	lemon juice	50 mL
2 tsp	curry powder	10 mL

* Soak and cook 1/2 cup (125 mL) of dried beans according to directions on pages 10 and 11.

- In large salad bowl, combine all ingredients except dressing.
- In tightly lidded jar, combine dressing ingredients. Shake well.
- Combine dressing with salad ingredients. Stir well.
- Cover and refrigerate until chilled. Keeps well for three days.

Serves 8-10.

Ginger Adzuki Salad

We have included four adzuki bean salads – each very different. These bright reddish beans provide good color contrast and seem happy to mate with practically any vegetable or rice. They are also available canned.

10	snow peas	10
10	asparagus spears, fresh or frozen	10
1 cup	cooked white rice	250 mL
1/2 cup	cooked adzuki beans	125 mL
1/2 cup	thinly sliced mushrooms	125 mL
1/4 cup	sliced almonds	50 mL
Dressing:		
2 Tbsp	vegetable oil	25 mL
3 Tbsp	orange juice	45 mL
1 Tbsp	red wine vinegar	15 mL
1	clove garlic, minced	1
1/2 tsp	ginger (more if desired)	3 mL
1/4 tsp	salt	1 mL

■ Wash and cut tips from snow peas. Steam them 1 minute. Cool, slice diagonally into 3 or 4 pieces according to size.

■ Cook asparagus until just tender. Cool. Slice into 3 or 4 pieces.

■ In medium bowl, place all the ingredients except the almonds and dressing.

■ In tightly lidded jar, combine dressing ingredients. Shake well. Add to salad.

■ Let stand in refrigerator at least one hour. Just before serving, add almonds. Toss. Serve in a bowl lined with greens.

Serves 4.

Warm Lentil & Peanut Salad

Here is another great recipe to win over the 'lentil shy' person. The combination of lentils and balsamic vinegar gives the dish a lively, earthy flavor. An electric frying pan makes this salad easy to prepare early in the day. A turn of the dial warms it up again.

1 cup	dried green/brown lentils	250 mL
6	strips bacon cut into	6
	1/2 " (1 cm) pieces	
3/4 cup	peanuts, coarsely chopped	175 mL
3/4 cup	thinly sliced green onions	175 mL
1/2 cup	chopped parsley	125 mL
Dressing:		
1/4 cup	balsamic vinegar	50 mL
1/4 cup	vegetable oil	50 mL
1 Tbsp	Dijon mustard	15 mL

■ Rinse and drain lentils. Place in saucepan covered with 3"(7.5 cm) of water. Bring to boil and reduce heat. Cover and simmer for 20 to 25 minutes until lentils are just tender. Drain and rinse. Set aside.

■ In large skillet, cook bacon until crisp. Turn off heat. Drain excess fat.

■ Add cooked lentils, nuts and green onions to bacon. Toss lightly.

■ In tightly lidded jar, combine dressing ingredients. Shake well.

■ Add dressing. Toss again. Serve warm, garnished with chopped parsley.

Serves 4-6.

Vegetable Lentil Salad

Lots of pluses with this salad – healthy, crunchy and tasty are just three. It also keeps very well, so it could be made a day or two ahead of planned entertaining.

3/4 cup	dried green/brown lentils	175 mL
2	carrots, thinly sliced	2
1 cup	cauliflower, cut in small flowerets	250 mL
1	medium red pepper, finely chopped	1
4	green onions, thinly sliced	4
Dressing:		
1/4 cup	vegetable oil	50 mL
1/4 cup	white wine vinegar	50 mL
1 tsp	dried oregano	5 mL
1 tsp	sugar	5 mL
	salt and pepper to taste	

- Cook 3/4 cup (175 mL) dried lentils according to directions on page 11. Drain and rinse.
- Place lentils in a salad bowl. Stir in vegetables.
- In tightly lidded jar, combine dressing ingredients. Shake well. Stir into lentil mixture.
- Refrigerate for a few hours to allow flavors to blend. Stir occasionally.

Serves 6.

Main Dishes

Main Dishes

Rainbow Chili

Vegetables from all over the colour spectrum meet in this wonderful chili. Because of the short cooking time, the colors stay bright and beautiful.

2 Tbsp	vegetable oil	25 mL
3	cloves garlic, minced	3
1	onion, chopped	1
I	large carrot, sliced	1
1 cup	sliced mushrooms	250 mL
1	red pepper, chopped	1
1	green pepper, chopped	1
1	can (28 oz/ 796 mL) diced tomatoes	1
3 cups	cooked black beans*	750 mL
1	jalapeno pepper, minced	1
1 Tbsp	chili powder	15 mL
1 tsp	ground cumin	5 mL
1 tsp	dried oregano	5 mL
1 tsp	salt	5 mL

* If using dried beans, soak and cook 1 1/4 cups (300 mL) according to directions on pages 10 and 11.

■ In a large saucepan, sauté garlic, onion, carrot, mushrooms and peppers in oil over medium heat for 5 minutes.

■ Stir in tomatoes, beans and jalapeno peppers. Simmer, uncovered, for 20 minutes.

■ Add seasonings and cook 5 minutes more. Serve in large bowls accompanied by whole grain buns.

Serves 4.

Three Bean Sausage Chili

If you like the hot variety of Italian sausage, go for it! This chili has been tested with both types. Our personal preference is the mild because of the recipe's added seasonings.

2 Tbsp	vegetable oil	25 mL
1/2 lb	mild Italian sausage, cut in 1/2"(1 cm) slices	225 g
1	medium onion, chopped	1
1	green pepper, chopped	1
2	cloves garlic, minced	2
1	jalapeno pepper, minced	1
1 cup	cooked romano beans	250 mL
1 cup	cooked red kidney beans	250 mL
1 cup	cooked black beans	250 mL
1	can (19 oz/540 mL) diced tomatoes	1
2 tsp	chili powder	10 mL
1 tsp	ground cumin	5 mL
1 tsp	dried oregano	5 mL

■ In a large saucepan, sauté sausage pieces in 1 Tbsp (15 mL) oil over medium heat until browned. Remove to a plate. Drain.

■ In remaining oil, sauté onion, pepper and garlic for 3 minutes.

■ Return sausages to saucepan, stir in beans and tomatoes. Simmer covered 20 minutes.

■ Add chili powder, cumin and oregano. Simmer 10 minutes more.

Serves 4.

Black & White Chili

Presentation in a black and white rimmed bowl makes this dish the winner of the 'Miss Bean America' contest. However, it's equally talented in the taste and speed-of-preparation category.

2 Tbsp	vegetable oil	25 mL
3	garlic cloves, minced	3
2	medium onions, chopped	2
2 cups	cooked navy beans*	500mL
2 cups	cooked black beans*	500 mL
1	can (28 oz/796 mL) diced tomatoes	1
1 Tbsp	chili powder	15 mL
2 tsp	ground cumin	10 mL
	salt and pepper to taste	

* If using dried beans, soak and cook 3/4 cups (175 mL) according to directions on pages 10 and 11.

■ In medium saucepan, sauté garlic and onions in oil over medium heat for 5 minutes.

■ Add remaining ingredients. Simmer 30 minutes.

■ Taste. Adjust seasonings.

Serves 4.

Pinto Bean Chili

A blue ribbon recipe for a group. Even if there are only a few people expected, try it anyway. It keeps well in the refrigerator and reheats easily in the microwave.

7 cups	cooked pinto beans*	1.75 L
3 Tbsp	vegetable oil	45 mL
2	large onions, chopped	2
4	cloves garlic, minced	4
1	can (28 oz/796 mL) tomatoes, chopped	1
1	can (12 oz/341 mL) kernel corn, drained	1
2	medium zucchini, cut lengthwise and cut in 1/4"(.5 cm) slices	2
1/4 cup	balsamic vinegar	50 mL
1 Tbsp	ground cumin	15 mL
2 tsp	dried oregano	10 mL
1 tsp	salt	5 mL
1 tsp	red pepper flakes	5 mL
1/2 tsp	freshly ground pepper	3 mL
	chopped green onions	
	parmesan cheese	

* Soak and cook 2 1/2 cups (625 mL) of dried pinto beans according to directions on pages 10 and 11.

- In a large pot, sauté onions and garlic in oil over medium heat for 5 minutes.
- Add tomatoes, corn, and zucchini. Simmer for 25 minutes.
- Add remaining ingredients and simmer 10 minutes more.
- Serve in bowls and sprinkle with chopped green onions and grated parmesan cheese.

Serves 8.

Autumn Chili

So called because the oranges and reds of the vegetables are the colors of fall leaves. Also, fresh pumpkin is readily available at this time. Substitute or increase amounts of other vegetables for the pumpkin when you make Autumn Chili the rest of the year.

2 Tbsp	vegetable oil	25 mL
1	large onion,chopped	1
3	cloves garlic, minced	3
1	large carrot, sliced	1
1 cup	peeled, cubed pumpkin	250 mL
1 cup	peeled, cubed squash*	250 mL
1 cup	peeled, cubed turnip	250 mL
2	parsnips, sliced	2
2 cups	cooked navy or Great Northern beans**	500 mL
1	can (28 oz/796 mL) tomatoes, chopped	1
1 Tbsp	chili powder	15 mL
1 tsp	ground cumin	5 mL
	salt to taste	

* Acorn or butternut squash work well.
** Soak and cook 3/4 cup (175 mL) dried beans according to directions on pages 10 and 11.

- In large saucepan, sauté onion and garlic in oil over medium heat for 3 minutes.
- Add remaining ingredients except seasonings. Simmer 20 minutes.
- Add chili and cumin. Simmer 15 minutes more. Adjust seasonings. Do not overcook. Vegetables should be firm.
- Serve in bowls accompanied by warmed crusty buns.

Serves 6.

Ben's Beans

Sometimes it's tough to introduce kids to beans. This one was gobbled up by a 10 year old hockey player named Ben. The truth is it's really a dressed up version of pork and beans. The adults at the table also gave it thumbs up.

1 Tbsp	vegetable oil	15 mL
1/2 lb	sausage, cut in 1/2 " (1 cm) slices	225 g
1	medium onion, chopped	1
2	cloves garlic, minced	2
1	green pepper, chopped	1
1	can (14 oz/398 mL) tomatoes, undrained and chopped	1
1	can (14 oz/ 398 mL) beans in tomato sauce	1
1 tsp	dried oregano	5 mL
1 tsp	dried basil	5 mL

- In skillet, brown sausage slices in oil for 5 minutes. Move to one side and brown the onion, green pepper and garlic. Drain excess fat.
- Add tomatoes and herbs. Simmer 10 minutes. Add beans in tomato sauce and simmer 3 minutes more.
- Serve in bowls accompanied by garlic bread.

Serves 3-4.

Black Bean Frittata

A chunk of cheese, a few eggs, a tomato in the refrigerator and you're ready for anything and anybody. And now that you're a bean convert you also have cartons of cooked beans. So, presto! – a frittata to impress your ever present dinner partner or the casual drop-in company!

1 Tbsp.	olive oil	15 mL
1/4 cup	onion, finely chopped	50 mL
1 cup	assorted peppers, chopped*	250 mL
1	tomato, chopped	1
1/3 cup	cooked black beans	75 mL
1/4 cup	grated cheese**	50 mL
4	eggs	4
2 Tbsp	milk	25 mL
	freshly ground pepper	

* Use any sweet peppers you have on hand.
** Any kind of cheese will work.

- Preheat oven to 300°F (140°C).
- In a 10 inch (25 cm) frying pan with an oven proof handle, sauté onion and peppers in oil over medium heat until soft, about 5 minutes.
- Add tomato, black beans and cheese.
- In a separate bowl, lightly beat eggs and add milk and pepper.
- Pour egg mixture into pan.
- Bake in oven for 10 to 15 minutes, until centre is set. Insert a knife into the middle to test for doneness - it should come out clean.

Serves 2.

Spanish Chicken

If you could compare food to clothing, this dish would be an elastic waisted skirt or pair of pants. In other words, it fits whatever size you want. Some feel a whole chicken breast is just right; others feel a half is adequate. For a crowd, it can be baked in the oven after the chicken, onion and garlic are browned.

2 Tbsp	olive oil	25 mL
3	whole chicken breasts, boned, skin removed	3
1	large onion, thinly sliced	1
3	cloves garlic, minced	3
3	tomatoes, chopped	3
1	green pepper, thinly sliced	1
1 tsp	dried marjoram	5 mL
1 tsp	dried basil	5 mL
1/2 tsp	crumbled dried red chili peppers*	3 mL
3/4 cup	canned chick peas (garbanzo beans) drained and rinsed	175 mL
1/2 cup	sliced black olives	125 mL
	salt and pepper to taste	
	cooked rice	

* More if desired.

- In large skillet, heat oil over medium heat. Brown chicken on both sides. Remove from pan.
- Add onion and garlic and sauté for 3 minutes.
- Return chicken to skillet. Add tomatoes, green pepper and seasonings. Simmer covered 20 minutes.
- Add chick peas and olives. Simmer 10 minutes more. Add salt and pepper to taste
- Serve over white or brown rice.

Serves 3-6.

Black Bean Stir-Fry

Stir-fry says 'fast' – this one also says 'spicy', 'tasty' and 'fit-for-company'. If, and it's a big if, you have leftovers, microwave them and serve in a warm pita pocket.

1	whole boneless, chicken breast, skin removed	1
1 Tbsp	chili powder	15 mL
1 Tbsp	ground cumin	15 mL
3 Tbsp	vegetable oil	45 mL
1	medium onion, thinly sliced	1
1	green pepper, thinly sliced	1
2	medium tomatoes, seeded & chopped	2
1/2 cup	cooked black beans	125 mL
3/4 cup	chicken stock*	175 mL
2 tsp	cornstarch	10 mL
	cooked rice	

*Can use bouillon cubes or instant granules. Follow package instructions.

- Slice chicken breast into very thin strips. This is much easier to do if your chicken is slightly frozen.

- In medium bowl, mix chili and cumin together. Roll chicken strips in these spices.

- In skillet, stir-fry chicken in oil until pink disappears. Add onion and pepper and cook 3 minutes. Add tomatoes and beans. Stir-fry 1 minute.

- Combine chicken stock and cornstarch. Add to skillet mixture.

- Cook 2 minutes more or until thickened.

- Serve over rice.

Serves 4.

Mexican Baked Beans

Chipotle (chee-poe-tlay) peppers give these baked beans their distinctive flavor. Hunt the peppers down in the Mexican section of your supermarket or in a specialty food store. These beans make a simple supper served with a salad. Use leftovers to make the Tex Mex Lunch on the next page.

1 Tbsp	vegetable oil	15 mL
1	medium onion, chopped	1
1	clove garlic, minced	1
1 1/2 cups	cooked black beans*	375 mL
1 1/2 cups	cooked pinto beans*	375 mL
1	canned chipotle pepper, finely chopped**	1
1 tsp	paprika	5 mL
1 tsp	chili powder	5 mL
1	can (7 1/2 oz/213 mL) tomato sauce	1
1/3 cup	red wine or water	75 mL
	lots of freshly ground pepper	

* If using dried beans, soak and cook 3/4 cup (175 mL) dried beans according to instructions on pages 10 and 11. Soak and cook each variety of bean separately.
** Chipotle peppers are roasted smoked jalapeno peppers. They come in cans in adobo sauce. After you open the can, transfer the contents to a jar with a tightly fitting lid. Store in refrigerator.

■ In skillet, sauté onion and garlic in oil over medium heat for 5 minutes.

■ In a medium sized casserole, combine all the ingredients.

■ Bake, covered, at 325⁰F (160⁰C) for 1 hour.

Serves 4.

Tex Mex Lunch

Another sneaky way to introduce young children to beans. No problem with teenagers either. This would also be perfect for a Friday night supper when everyone is off and running.

4	medium-size flour tortillas	4
1 1/2 cups	Mexican Baked Beans*	375 mL
2	medium tomatoes, chopped	2
4	green onions, chopped	4
1 cup	grated mozzarella or cheddar cheese	250 mL

* Recipe on opposite page.

- Place tortillas on a lightly greased cookie sheet.
- Spread 1/4 of the Mexican Baked Beans on each tortilla.
- Cover with chopped tomatoes. Sprinkle with green onions and top with cheese.
- Bake at 350⁰F (180⁰C) for 10 minutes or until cheese melts.

Serves 4.

Mediterranean Black-Eyed Peas

If you love healthy, low fat food with no flavor sacrifice, look no further. The combination of turmeric, cumin and coriander is the spicy kick. As an accompaniment, treat yourself to a wonderful specialty bread at your local bakery.

2 Tbsp	vegetable oil	25 mL
2	cloves garlic, minced	2
1	medium onion, chopped	1
1	red pepper, cut in strips	1
6	mushrooms, sliced	6
4	fresh tomatoes, peeled and chopped*	4
1/2 cup	sliced black olives	125 mL
1 cup	cooked black-eyed peas**	250 mL
1 tsp	ground cumin	5 mL
1 tsp	ground coriander	5 mL
1/2 tsp	turmeric	3 mL
	salt to taste	
	chopped cilantro or parsley	

* Can substitute one (19 oz/540 mL) can.
**If using dried beans, cook 1/2 cup (125 mL) as directed on page 11.

- In skillet, sauté garlic, onion, pepper strips and mushrooms in oil over medium heat for 5 minutes.
- Add tomatoes. Cover and simmer 10 minutes.
- Add remaining ingredients. Simmer 10 minutes more.
- If tomatoes do not produce enough liquid, add tomato juice. Taste. Adjust seasonings.
- Serve over couscous or rice.
- Garnish with chopped cilantro or parsley.

Serves 4.

Sunny Orange Beans

This dish is bright in color and light in taste. The solution to the dilemma of wanting beans for dinner but also wanting room for a large decadent dessert.

1 Tbsp	olive oil	15 mL
1	medium onion, chopped	1
1	green pepper, chopped	1
1	red pepper, chopped	1
1	can (14 oz/396 mL) tomato sauce	1
3/4 cup	orange juice	175 mL
1/2 cup	water	125 mL
	grated rind of 1 orange	
2 tsp	paprika	10 mL
2 tsp	Worcestershire sauce	10 mL
	several dashes pepper sauce	
1 cup	cooked navy beans*	250 mL
	cooked rice	

* If using dried beans, soak and cook 1/2 cup (125 mL) according to directions on pages 10 and 11.

■ In medium saucepan, sauté onion and peppers in oil over medium heat for 5 minutes.

■ Add remaining ingredients and simmer covered for 15 minutes.

■ Serve over rice.

Serves 4.

Beans on a Bun

This recipe could be subtitled 'Beans on the Run'. Short of pizza delivery it's hard to imagine anything quicker. Another favorite of children – they can even make it themselves.

1 lb	lean ground beef	450 g
1	medium onion, chopped	1
1	green or red pepper, chopped	1
1	can (19 oz/540 mL) red kidney or pinto beans, drained and rinsed	1
1 1/2 cups	salsa	375 mL
4	hamburger buns, split in half and toasted	4
	Monterey Jack or cheddar cheese, grated	

■ In skillet, sauté ground beef, onion and pepper over medium heat until meat is no longer pink.

■ Stir in salsa and beans and simmer over low heat for 15 minutes, stirring occasionally.

■ Spoon bean mixture on toasted buns. Sprinkle with grated cheese. Broil for 1 minute or until cheese melts.

Serves 4.

Tamale Pie

This is a very filling family dinner. It's difficult to say exactly how many it feeds. Three hungry testers devoured it all but normally, four people should be satisfied. A mixture of greens dressed with a light vinaigrette is a suitable companion.

1 Tbsp	vegetable oil	15 mL
1	medium onion, chopped	1
2	cloves garlic, minced	2
1	medium green pepper, chopped	1
2 tsp	chili powder	10 mL
1/2 tsp	ground cumin	3 mL
1	can (19 oz/540 mL) kidney beans*	1
1/2 cup	corn, frozen or canned	125 mL
1	can (7 oz/213 mL) tomato sauce	1
1/3 cup	grated cheddar cheese	75 mL
Topping:		
3/4 cup	cornmeal	175 mL
1 1/2 cups	milk (skim is fine)	375 mL
1 Tbsp	vegetable oil	15 mL
1	egg	1
1/2 tsp	salt	2 mL

* Can substitute pinto beans, if desired.

- In large saucepan, sauté onion, garlic and green pepper in oil over medium heat for 5 minutes.
- Add remaining filling ingredients except cheese and topping. Simmer, covered, for 15 minutes.
- Place in 8"x 8" (20 cm x 20 cm) baking pan. Sprinkle with cheese.

To prepare topping:

- In a medium saucepan, combine all topping ingredients. Mix well. Cook 5 minutes or until thickened. Stir constantly.
- Cover bean mixture with topping. Bake at 350⁰F (180⁰ C) until crust is done, about 30 minutes.

Serves 4-6.

Pesto Fettucine With Beans

Two time honoured staples – pasta and beans – combine with prepared pesto sauce. As a colorful alternative to the standard basil based pesto try the sundried tomato variety. Look for it in bottles on the specialty food section of your supermarket.

2 Tbsp	vegetable oil	25 mL
1	medium onion, chopped finely	1
2	cloves garlic, minced	2
1 cup	vegetable stock*	250 mL
1	can (19 oz/540 mL) white kidney beans, drained and rinsed	1
1 lb	fettucine	450g
1 cup	prepared pesto sauce	250 mL
	salt and pepper to taste	
	freshly grated parmesan cheese	
	toasted pine nuts**	

* Can use bouillon cubes or instant granules. Follow package instructions. Recipe for vegetable stock on page 56.
** To toast pine nuts: Place them on a baking sheet. Bake in 325⁰F (165⁰C) for 5 to 8 minutes or until light brown. Watch them very closely as they can darken quickly.

- In skillet, sauté onion and garlic in oil over medium heat for 3 minutes.

- Reduce heat and add vegetable stock and drained beans. Simmer 5 minutes.

- Meanwhile, cook fettucine according to package directions. Drain.

- Place in heated serving bowl. Add pesto and hot bean mixture. Toss well.

- Sprinkle with toasted pine nuts and parmesan.

Serves 4.

Pasta & Ceci

Ceci is the Italian name for garbanzo beans or chick peas. This authentic recipe was given to us by an Italian friend. It is so easy to make it's hard to believe it's so good.

2 Tbsp	olive oil	25 mL
1	medium onion, chopped	1
1	can (19 oz/540 mL) crushed tomatoes	1
3 Tbsp	chopped fresh oregano*	45 mL
1	can (19 oz/540 mL) chick peas, (garbanzo beans) drained and rinsed	1
	salt and freshly ground pepper to taste	
1/2 lb	pasta**	225 mL
	freshly grated parmesan cheese	

* If fresh oregano is not available, you can use 1 Tbsp of dried oregano.
**Use spaghetti broken into 2 to 3 inch pieces, unless you can find "medium to large ditali" or "rigati", the pasta called for in the recipe. We have not found these to be readily available.

- In saucepan, sauté onion in oil over medium heat until soft.
- Add tomatoes and oregano. Simmer for 15 minutes. Add chick peas and simmer for 5 minutes more.
- While sauce is simmering, cook pasta in boiling water according to directions. Drain.
- Add sauce to pasta. Stir gently. Serve in individual bowls or plates and top with parmesan cheese.

Serves 3.

Fajitas

If your family is in the mood for 'bonding', this is the meal for you. Take the skillet off the stove, pop it on the table (using a hot mat of course!) and let everyone make their own.

2 Tbsp	vegetable oil	25 mL
1	red onion, sliced vertically	1
1	green pepper, cut in strips	1
1	red pepper, cut in strips	1
2	cloves garlic, minced	2
1 tsp	ground cumin	5 mL
1 tsp	chili powder	5 mL
1 Tbsp	lime juice	15 mL
1 tsp	chipotle pepper in adobo sauce,* finely chopped	5 mL
1 cup	cooked black beans**	250 mL
4	10"(25 cm) flour tortillas	4
	sour cream	
	salsa	

* optional
** If using dried beans, soak and cook 1/2 cup (125 mL) according to directions on pages 10 and 11.

- In wok or large skillet, sauté onion, peppers and garlic in oil over medium heat for 5 minutes.
- Add remaining ingredients and heat through - 3 to 5 minutes.
- While you are cooking the filling, wrap tortillas in foil. Warm in 350°F (180°C) until filling is ready.
- To serve, put tortillas on a large plate or in a basket. Bring wok or skillet to table and place on a hot mat.
- Let everyone serve themselves by placing the filling along the middle of a tortilla and adding sour cream and salsa as desired. The tortilla is then rolled and eaten in your hands.

Makes 4 fajitas.

Southern Lasagne

When you're cooking for a crowd, try this recipe instead of the usual lasagne. The Cajun seasoning – found in the spice section – gives it a real lift.

1	can (28 oz/796 mL) crushed tomatoes	1
1/2 cup	water	125 mL
2 tsp	Cajun seasoning	10 mL
1 tsp	ground cumin	5 mL
1	clove garlic, minced	1
1 Tbsp	olive oil	15 mL
1 each	green & red pepper, chopped	1 each
1	medium zucchini, chopped	1
1	medium onion, chopped	1
8	medium mushrooms, chopped	8
1	can (14 oz/398 mL) black beans, drained and rinsed	1
1 1/2 cups	niblet corn	375 mL
8-10	8" (20 cm) flour tortillas	8-10
1 1/2 cups	grated cheese, (jalapeno Monterey Jack is nice)	375 mL

■ Combine first 5 ingredients in a saucepan and simmer 10 minutes.

■ Sauté vegetables (except corn) in oil over medium heat for 5 minutes.

■ Combine black beans and corn.

■ *To assemble:* put 1/3 of the tomato sauce in a lightly greased 9"x 13" (22 x 33 cm) baking dish. Cover with 1/2 of black bean mixture. Then place one layer of whole tortillas on top. Cut pieces to fill any spaces. Add another 1/3 of tomato sauce.

■ Cover with the sautéed vegetables and top with 2/3 of the cheese.

■ Place another layer of tortillas, the rest of the black bean mixture and a final layer of tortillas.

■ Top with the rest of the tomato sauce and cheese. Bake at 350°F (180°C) for 30 minutes.

Serves 8.

Snowbird Beans

A favorite with those who flee northern winters for the ease of Arizona and Florida. The aroma of this dish wafting through the warm air reminds them of their suffering friends.

2 Tbsp	vegetable oil	25 mL
1	large onion, chopped	1
1	green pepper, chopped	1
3	stalks celery, chopped	3
1	can (19 oz/540 mL) kidney beans, drained rinsed	1
1	pkg (16 oz/500 g) frozen lima beans, thawed	1
1	can (14 oz/398 mL) beans in tomato sauce	1
1	can (14 oz/ 398 mL) chopped tomatoes	1
1/4 cup	white vinegar	50 mL
2 Tbsp	brown sugar	25 mL
1 Tbsp	prepared mustard	15 mL
1 tsp	dry mustard	5 mL
2	dashes pepper sauce	2
3	dashes Worcestershire sauce	3
	salt and pepper to taste	

■ In large oven proof pot, sauté onion, green peppers and celery in oil over medium heat for 5 minutes.

■ Add beans and tomatoes.

■ In small bowl, mix remaining ingredients. Add to the bean and tomato mixture. Stir well.

■ Bake, covered, in 325ºF (180ºC) oven for 1 hour.

■ Remove lid. Stir. Cook 15 to 20 minutes more or until thickened.

Serves 6.

Black Beans in Spicy Sauce

Salsa – it's handy and versatile. Not just a dip for tortilla chips these days but a cupboard must. The mild variety – because of the added spices and oregano – should be hot enough for this sauce.

1 tsp	olive oil	5 mL
1/4 cup	onion, finely chopped	50 mL
1	clove garlic, minced	1
1 cup	cooked black beans*	250 mL
1	can (14 oz/398 mL) diced tomatoes	1
1/4 cup	salsa	50 mL
1/2 tsp	ground cumin	3 mL
1/2 tsp	chili powder	3 mL
1/2 tsp	dried oregano	3 mL
3/4 cup	orzo**	250 mL
	grated cheddar or Monterey Jack cheese	

* If using dried beans, soak and cook 1/2 cup (125 mL) according to directions on pages 10 and 11.
** Orzo is a small pasta that looks like rice.

■ In a medium saucepan, sauté onion and garlic in oil, over medium heat for 5 minutes. Add all other ingredients except orzo and cheese. Simmer, covered for 20 minutes.

■ While sauce is cooking, add orzo to 5 cups of boiling water. Cook uncovered for 10 minutes. Drain.

■ To serve, put orzo in shallow bowls. Top with spicy sauce and sprinkle with grated cheese.

Serves 2.

Bean Wrap Ups

*The newest healthy fast food is called Roll Ups or Wrap Ups.
They are hand-held tortillas eaten hot or cold. Their fillings are
totally flexible. Suggested ingredients could be refried beans,
salsa, grated cheese, small chicken pieces, any chili (not runny),
rice, sprouts, lettuce and any type of flavored mayonnaise. Here's
one Wrap Up we enjoy.*

8" or 10" (20 or 25 cm) tortillas, as many as necessary
- black refried beans (canned, or recipe page 109.)
- chunky salsa, purchased or page 18.
- grated Monterey Jack cheese
- flavored mayonnaise

To assemble:

■ On a tortilla, place ingredients down centre of wrap. Spread a thin
layer of mayonnaise on top of the ingredients.

■ Fold wrap up from the bottom about 2 inches. Press gently to
create a crease.

■ Hold in place with fingers of one hand, then fold in left side of
wrap to cover the filling.

■ Roll the wrap over to encase filling on all sides. Wrap the
bottom quarter with a napkin and microwave about 2 minutes
or until ingredients are warm.

■ You can also wrap them completely in foil and place on a baking
sheet. Heat in a 325⁰F (160⁰C) oven for 10 minutes or until warm.

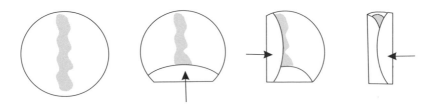

Black Bean Fish Bake

Works well with any available white fish fillets. Especially speedy if you prepare the topping the day before. Serve with rice and a green salad. Good for the family or for company.

1 lb.	white fish fillets	450 g
Topping:		
1/2 cup	green onions, chopped	125 mL
2	tomatoes, diced	2
1	can (4 oz/114 mL) diced green chilies	1
1/4 cup	cilantro, finely chopped	50 mL
1/2 cup	cooked black beans	125 mL
	juice of 1 lime	

- In small bowl mix all topping ingredients.
- Lay fish fillets side by side in baking dish. Spoon topping evenly over fish.
- Bake, uncovered, at 375⁰F (190⁰C) for 20 to 30 minutes or until fish flakes. Drain any excess fluid.
- <u>Or,</u> this dish can also be microwaved, covered, for 5 to 7 minutes.
- Serve with lime wedges.

Serves 4.

Lamb & White Bean Stew

This stew is worth making a dent in your weekly food budget. The stewing part of the lamb is the most reasonable. This is a complete meal in one dish as the beans replace potatoes or rice.

2 lbs	lamb stew, cut in 1" (2.5 cm) cubes	900 g
2 Tbsp	flour	25 mL
3 Tbsp	vegetable oil	45 mL
1	medium onion, chopped	1
3	garlic cloves, minced	3
1 Tbsp	dried rosemary	15 mL
1 1/2 cups	beef or vegetable stock*	375 mL
3	bay leaves	3
2	carrots, cut in rounds	2
1 cup	cooked navy or Great Northern beans**	250 mL
3/4 cup	frozen green peas, thawed	175 mL
	salt and pepper to taste	

* Can use bouillon cubes or instant granules. Follow package directions. Recipe for vegetable stock on page 56.
** If using dried beans, soak and cook 1/2 cup (125 mL) according to directions on pages 10 and 11.

- Trim any excess fat from lamb with a sharp knife. Cut larger pieces into cubes. Dredge with flour. In a large skillet brown lamb cubes in oil over medium heat. Remove to oven proof casserole.

- Add more oil to skillet if necessary and brown onion, garlic and rosemary. Scrape all bits off pan. Add to browned lamb.

- Stir in stock and bay leaves. Place in oven and cook, covered, at 325⁰F (160⁰C) for 1 to 1 1/2 hours, or until lamb is tender.

- Add carrots and beans. Cook, covered, another 20 minutes.

- Taste and adjust seasonings. Remove bay leaves.

- Add thawed peas. Cook 10 minutes more.

- Thicken with a little flour if necessary.

Serves 4.

Vegetables & Side Dishes

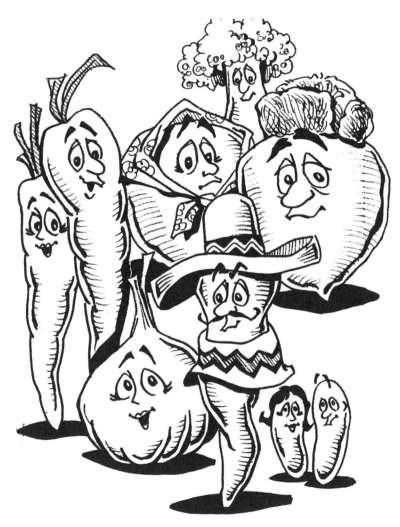

Vegetables & Side Dishes

Zucchini Bake

A very flexible family standby. Substitute any leftover or frozen beans you have on hand. Be creative with the seasoning if you don't have fine herbs.

1 Tbsp	olive oil	15 mL
1	medium white onion, thinly sliced	1
3	medium tomatoes, thinly sliced	3
2	medium zucchini, thinly sliced	2
3/4 cup	cooked black beans	175 mL
1 tsp	fine herbs	5 mL
1/3 cup	grated cheese	75 mL
	salt and pepper to taste	
Cornmeal Topping:		
1/2 cup	cornmeal	125 mL
1 cup	milk	250 mL
2 tsp	vegetable oil	10 mL
1/2 tsp	salt	2 mL
1	egg	1

* Can use an 8 1/2 oz (225 g) package of corn muffin mix

- Lightly oil a 8"x 8" pan.
- Using 1/2 the vegetables, place a thin layer of onions, followed by a layer of tomatoes, and a layer of zucchini.
- Sprinkle 1/2 the fine herbs and then all the black beans on this layer.
- Using the remaining vegetables make another layer each of onion, tomatoes and zucchini.
- Sprinkle with the rest of the fine herbs and the salt and pepper. Cover lightly with cheese. Top with Cornmeal Topping.

Cormeal Topping:

- In saucepan, combine all topping ingredients. Stirring constantly, heat over medium heat until thickened. Pour on vegetables immediately.
- Bake at 350°F (180°C) for 40 minutes.

Serves 6.

Refried Black Beans

Usually refried beans are made with kidney or pinto beans. The black bean version is gaining popularity. In this cookbook it is used in two appetizers, Mini Nachos and Layered Mexican Appetizer, as well as the Bean Wrap Ups in the Main Dish section. Can accompany any Mexican dish.

3 Tbsp	vegetable oil	45 mL
1	medium onion, finely chopped	1
1	jalapeno pepper*, minced	1
3	cloves garlic, minced	3
1 tsp	ground cumin	5 mL
1	can (19 oz/540 mL) black beans, drained and rinsed	1
1	large ripe tomato, peeled and chopped	1
1 tsp	salt	5 mL
	pepper to taste	

* Can substitute canned jalapeno peppers.

■ In medium skillet, sauté onion, jalapeno pepper, garlic and cumin in oil for 10 to 15 minutes or until very soft.

■ Add beans, tomatoes, salt and pepper. While mixture cooks, mash with the back of a large spoon or a potato masher. The consistency can be either chunky or completely smooth. If it seems dry, add a little more oil or warm water.

Yields 2 cups (500 mL).

Hoppin' Jack

This black-eyed pea and rice dish is a nod to the traditional southern Hoppin' John. It's a fresher, lighter version. We've tested it with thyme and substituted a red pepper for the tomato – just as tasty.

1 cup	cooked black-eyed peas*	250 mL
1/2 cup	uncooked white rice	125 mL
3	green onions, sliced	3
1/4 cup	chopped fresh basil	50 mL
1	tomato, seeds & pulp removed, diced	1
	salt and pepper	

* If using dried beans soak and cook 1/2 cup (125 mL) according to directions on pages 10 and 11.

- If using canned black-eyed peas, drain and rinse.
- In medium saucepan, cook rice according to package directions. When rice is cooked, add remaining ingredients. Stir and heat through. Serve at once.

Serves 4.

Black-Eyed Peas & Vegetables

This recipe is from scratch but is easily made with a can of black-eyed peas. Just rinse them and add a little vegetable stock with the sautéed ingredients. The flavors are subtle so it's a flexible companion for other dishes.

3/4 cup	dried black-eyed peas	175 mL
3 1/2 cups	vegetable stock*	875 mL
3	bay leaves	3
2 Tbsp	vegetable oil	25 mL
2	cloves garlic, minced	2
2	carrots, sliced lengthwise and then in thin rounds	2
1	medium onion, finely chopped	1
1	pepper, any color, cut in thin strips	1
1 tsp	paprika	5 mL
2 tsp	dried thyme	10 mL
	salt and pepper to taste	

* Can use bouillon cubes or instant granules. Follow package directions. Recipe for vegetable stock on page 56.

- In medium saucepan, simmer black-eyed peas with vegetable stock and bay leaves for 20 minutes, or until peas are tender but firm. Discard bay leaves.

- While peas are cooking, in large skillet sauté the remaining ingredients in oil over medium heat for 5 minutes.

- Add vegetable mixture to cooked peas. Mix well. Consistency should be moist but not runny.

- Serve immediately.

Serves 4.

Piquant Black-Eyed Peas

A very quick dish if you have a can of black-eyed peas on your shelf. Goes well with sliced meat.

1	can (14oz/398 mL) black-eyed peas,* drained and rinsed	1
2	green onions, sliced	2
Sauce:		
2 Tbsp	cider vinegar	25 mL
1 tsp	dry mustard	5 mL
1/2 tsp	sugar	3 mL
1	clove garlic, minced	1

* If using dried beans, cook 3/4 cup (175 mL) according to directions on page 11.

- Place black-eyed peas and green onions in a small saucepan.
- Mix sauce ingredients together. Pour into saucepan with peas and onions and stir well.
- Gently heat, stirring so that sauce coats the beans well. Serve immediately.

Serves 2-3.

Carrots, Squash & Chick Peas

The subtle taste of reduction is one of our healthy food trends. Instead of richly saucing a vegetable, gently simmer away the excess cooking liquid leaving the concentrated flavors.

1 Tbsp	vegetable oil	15 mL
1	medium onion, chopped	1
2	carrots, thinly sliced	2
2 cups	squash, cubed*	500 mL
1 cup	vegetable stock**	250 mL
1 tsp	ground coriander	5 mL
1/2 tsp	turmeric	3 mL
1/2 cup	chick peas (garbanzo beans), drained and rinsed	125 mL
	salt to taste	

* Use any squash similiar to an acorn squash.
** Can use bouillon cubes or granules. Follow package directions. Recipe for vegetable stock on page 56.

- In a medium saucepan, sauté onion in oil over medium heat for 3 minutes.
- Add carrots, squash and vegetable stock. Cook, covered, 10 minutes.
- Add seasonings and chick peas. Simmer, uncovered, for 3 to 5 minutes more or until vegetables are just tender. The stock will be reduced to a sauce-like consistency.

Serves 4.

Beans & Greens

Definitely a dish for those who feel most comfortable with a bean/cabbage combination. A longtime favorite for group dinners when everyone wants to help at the last minute, this stir-fry is an easily assigned task.

3 Tbsp	vegetable oil	45 mL
1	onion, finely chopped	1
2	cloves garlic, minced	2
2 cups	finely chopped green cabbage	500 mL
1/2 cup	cooked kidney beans	125 mL
1/2 tsp	paprika	3 mL
1/2 tsp	dried thyme	3 mL
	salt and pepper to taste	

- In skillet, sauté onion and garlic in oil over medium heat for 2 minutes.
- Add remaining ingredients and stir-fry 5 to 7 minutes more.
- Serve immediately.

Serves 4.

Lentil Pilaf

Lentils are wonderfully simple – no soaking required. But do peek into the pot at the 20 minute mark and every minute or so after, as they can quickly overcook. The lemon juice and tomatoes freshen their earthy flavor.

1 cup	dried green/brown lentils	250 mL
2 cups	vegetable stock*	500 mL
3	bay leaves	3
2 Tbsp	vegetable oil	25 mL
1/2	red pepper, finely chopped	1/2
1	carrot, thinly sliced	1
2	stalks celery, diced	2
4	green onions, thinly sliced	4
1 cup	canned tomatoes and juice, chopped	250 mL
1 Tbsp	lemon juice	15 mL
	salt and pepper to taste	

* Can use bouillon cubes or instant granules. Follow package directions. Recipe for vegetable stock on page 56.

- Rinse lentils well. Place in medium saucepan with vegetable stock and bay leaves. Cover and simmer for 20 to 25 minutes until lentils are tender but not mushy or dry.

- Drain and rinse lentils. Discard bay leaves. Return to saucepan.

- In skillet, sauté all vegetables except tomatoes in oil over medium heat for 3-5 minutes or until tender crisp.

- Add sautéed vegetables and tomatoes to cooked lentils. Stir in lemon juice and season to taste. Heat through.

Serves 4-6.

Red Cabbage Stir-Fry

Crunch, color, and bite are three descriptive words for this speedy vegetable side dish.

3 Tbsp	vegetable oil	45 mL
1	medium onion, finely chopped	1
2 cups	shredded red cabbage	500 mL
1 cup	cooked navy or Great Northern beans*	250 mL
1/3 cup	white vinegar	75 mL
2 Tbsp	brown sugar	25 mL

* If using dried beans, soak and cook 1/2 cup (125 mL) acccording to directions on pages 10 and 11.

■ In a small bowl, combine vinegar and brown sugar.

■ In large skillet, sauté onion in oil over medium heat for 2 minutes. Add cabbage and beans and stir-fry another 4 minutes.

■ Add vinegar brown sugar mixture. Cook 2 minutes more. Serve immediately.

Serves 4.

Lemony Garlic Limas

Many people remember lima beans from their childhood as too big, mealy and dry. If you have shied away from this wonderful bean, this is the introductory recipe for you. Definitely use frozen limas – they are smaller and green. The fresh lemon juice is the refreshingly light secret.

1 cup	frozen lima beans	250 mL
1/2 cup	frozen or canned niblet corn	125 mL
Dressing:		
3 Tbsp	vegetable oil	45 mL
2 Tbsp	fresh lemon juice	25 mL
1	clove garlic, minced	1
	salt and pepper to taste	

■ In medium saucepan, simmer lima beans and frozen corn in small amount of water according to package directions. If using a can of niblet corn, drain and add to the cooked, drained limas.

■ Mix dressing ingredients together.

■ Drain vegetables and stir in dressing. Heat through. Serve immediately.

Serves 2.

Ratatouille

Ratatouille is a rich and hearty melange of favorite Mediterranan ingredients. Don't be shy about using lots of garlic and herbs – the long cooking mellows their flavors. It is great served as a vegetable or can be party fare when served over pasta.

2 Tbsp	olive oil	25 mL
2	cloves garlic, minced	2
1	large eggplant, cut in half and sliced	1
2	medium zucchini, sliced	2
1	large onion, sliced	1
1	large green pepper, sliced	1
1	large red pepper, sliced	1
1	can (19 oz/540 mL) crushed tomatoes	1
1 cup	cooked navy beans*	250 mL
1 Tbsp	dried basil	15 mL
2 tsp	dried oregano	10 mL
	freshly ground pepper	

* If using dried beans, soak and cook 1/2 cup (125 mL) according to directions on pages 10 and 11.

- Combine oil and garlic in the bottom of a large casserole.
- Place a layer of eggplant, followed by layers of zucchini, onions and the combined peppers.
- Top the layers of vegetables with half the tomatoes, beans, herbs and ground pepper.
- Repeat layers of vegetables. Add remaining tomatoes, beans, herbs and ground pepper.
- Cover and cook in oven at 325°F (160°C) for 1 hour. Stir occasionally. (Don't be afraid to mix the vegetables up).
- This may also be simmered gently on the stove top, in a large saucepan.

Serves 8 as a vegetable.
Serves 6 as a main dish over pasta.

Stuffed Tomatoes – Two Ways

It was a dead heat with the testers – half favored #1, half, #2. You can mix and match the fillings with the peppers on the next page.

# 1: For 4 firm medium to large tomatoes:		
1 cup	cooked brown rice	250 mL
1/2 cup	cooked black beans	125 mL
1/2 cup	shredded Monterey Jack cheese	125 mL
1 tsp	ground cumin	5 mL
4	green onions, sliced	4
# 2: For 4 firm medium to large tomatoes:		
1 cup	cooked bulgar wheat*	250 mL
1/2 cup	cooked chick peas (garbanzo beans)	125 mL
4	green onions, sliced	4
1 Tbsp	vegetable oil	15 mL
2 tsp	lemon juice	10 mL
	the tomato pulp, chopped	
	salt and pepper to taste	

* Place 1/2 cup (125 mL) of bulgar wheat in a bowl and pour boiling water to cover by at least 1" (2.5cm). Let stand for 1/2 hour until water has been absorbed. Drain any excess.

■ Scoop the pulp and seeds from the tomatoes. Invert and drain on paper towels. Reserve tomato pulp for second version.

■ In a small bowl, mix together either version. Generously fill the tomatoes.

■ Place filled tomatoes in a baking dish with 1/4" (.5 cm) water. Cover. Bake 325⁰F (160⁰C) for 20 to 25 minutes. Don't overcook.

Serves 4.

Stuffed Peppers

It has been fascinating to watch the evolution of cooking times of the pepper. Back in the dark ages, you simmered them for 20 minutes before filling them. Even in these enlightened times, recipes still contain a 3 minute pre-simmer instruction. The good news is you don't have to precook the peppers at all! It's difficult to give accurate measurements for the filling as peppers vary so much in size. Decrease or increase the rice or beans as necessary.

2	red, green or yellow peppers	2
1/2 cup	cooked white rice	125 mL
1/2 cup	cooked red kidney beans	125 mL
1	green onion, finely sliced	1
1	jalapeno pepper, finely diced*	1/2
1/2 tsp	chili powder	3 mL
1/4 cup	shredded cheddar cheese	50 mL

* Can substitute 2 Tbsp (25 mL) diced canned green chilies.

- Slice peppers VERTICALLY so that you have four halves. Remove seeds and membrane.
- In small bowl, mix remaining ingredients.
- Fill peppers. Place them in an ovenproof pan with 1/4" (.5 cm) of water. Cover with a lid or tin foil.
- Bake at 325⁰F (160⁰C) for 25 minutes. Serve immediately.

Serves 2-4.

Index

About The Authors

*Trish Ross and Jacquie Trafford live in British Columbia, Canada's most western province. Since the success of their first book, **Easy Beans**, which was published in 1994, Trish and Jacquie have been testing and researching new combinations for legumes, all the while testing them on their respective families and friends. This all-new cookbook is the result of many discoveries made in their travels, combined with lots of time spent in the kitchen.*

Order Form

Please send me:

_____ copies of *More Easy Beans* at $15.00 Cdn ($12.00 US) per book (price includes taxes and shipping).

_____ copies of *Easy Beans* (our first bean cookbook) at $15.00 Cdn ($12.00 US) per book (price includes taxes and shipping).

NUMBER OF BOOKS _____ X $ _____ = _____

TOTAL ENCLOSED = _____

NAME_____

STREET_____

CITY _____ PROV/STATE _____

POSTAL CODE/ZIP _____ PHONE _____

Please make the cheque or money order payable to: Big Bean Publishing and mail to:
    Big Bean Publishing
    RR2, Site 4 C58
    Chase, BC Canada V0E 1M0

Order Form

Please send me:

_____ copies of *More Easy Beans* at $15.00 Cdn ($12.00 US) per book (price includes taxes and shipping).

_____ copies of *Easy Beans* (our first bean cookbook) at $15.00 Cdn ($12.00 US) per book (price includes taxes and shipping).

NUMBER OF BOOKS _____ X $ _____ = _____

TOTAL ENCLOSED = _____

NAME_____

STREET_____

CITY _____ PROV/STATE _____

POSTAL CODE/ZIP _____ PHONE _____

Please make the cheque or money order payable to: Big Bean Publishing and mail to:
    Big Bean Publishing
    RR2, Site 4 C58
    Chase, BC Canada V0E 1M0